MW00717114

Family Likeness

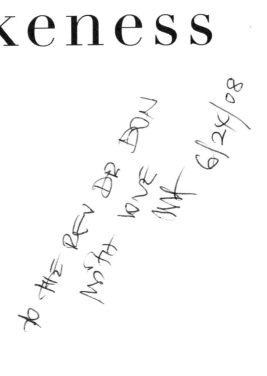

Family
Likeness

Wilson Awasu

WINEPRESS WP PUBLISHING

© 2008 by Wilson Awasu. All rights reserved.

WinePress Publishing (PO Box 428, Enumclaw, WA 98022) functions only as book publisher. As such, the ultimate design, content, editorial accuracy, and views expressed or implied in this work are those of the author.

No part of this publication may be reproduced, stored in a retrieval system, or transmitted in any way by any means—electronic, mechanical, photocopy, recording, or otherwise—without the prior permission of the copyright holder, except as provided by USA copyright law.

All Scripture quotations unless otherwise indicated are taken from the *Holy Bible: Revised Standard Version.* Copyright © 1972 Thomas Nelson, Inc. Used by permission. All rights reserved.

ISBN 13: 978-1-57921-927-7
ISBN 10: 1-57921-927-6
Library of Congress Catalog Card Number: 2007934242

CONTENTS

Introduction:
When Amazing
Parallels Occur

I tell you, friends," Jesus said. "Anyone who believes in me will do the same works I've done, and even greater works, because I'm going to be with the Father." Then he issued a blank check. "Ask anything in my name. And I'll do it" (John 14:12–13).

"Anyone" includes Peter and John, Mary Magdalene and Philip, Barnabas and Paul, Priscilla and Aquila, and you and me. So does "anything." It also takes into account their prayers and ours. Why? Jesus said so. He wants even God-defiant people, Satan, and demons to see, feel, and taste that God's life in ordinary people produces a family likeness.

A family likeness means that members of a family share some characteristics, knowledge, and priorities. Having a family likeness with God's family means that God's family members will be aligned with God and his priorities, just like Jesus was. Like him, they become channels of God's love, forgiveness, peace, joy, life, freedom, and wholeness to people and situations needing them. Here are some examples of demonstrations of family likeness—doing things that show one is a member of God's family.

Exorcism

A demoniac once met Jesus. The demons Jesus evicted from him filled two thousand pigs. The pigs ran amok and drowned in a nearby lake. The demoniac instantly returned to sanity (Mark 5:1–20).

In a similar way, Kelly experienced sanity at the Adolphus Hotel in Dallas, Texas. Right after a speaker had finished talking to a hundred delegates of a Campus Crusade evangelistic conference in a conference room, Kelly got up and walked toward the podium. She collapsed in the center aisle. Four men picked her up and helped her out into the hallway. I invited myself and approached them.

When I got to where they sat her, I heard the men ask Kelly about drug use, hunger, exhaustion, etc. She sat mute, defiant, and weird-looking.

"Ask her to tell you her name. Demonic looks often have substance to them," I said three times, unheeded.

After a while, Bill, one of the men assisting her, asked Kelly, "What's your name?"

A guttural voice spoke something none of us understood. Scared to reality, Kelly's helpers relocated her to a guest room. I followed, uninvited. For the next two hours, Kelly's helpers tried and failed to evict Kelly's "guttural" invader.

Then Bill turned to me and said, "Wilson, why aren't you praying with us for Kelly?"

"I want to, Bill," I said, "but I don't know what to pray." *It's one thing to discern a demonic presence, but it's another to know what to do to evict it,* I wanted to add. I thought this was obvious, so I said nothing.

We waited in silence for thirty minutes. Then I discerned that Kelly's invader was a spirit guide she'd contacted through an occult initiation. I shared that with Bill and the others, and using that information, I ordered the spirit guide away in Jesus' name.

"I'm free, I'm free," Kelly jumped up and said before I said amen to my prayer.

And she was indeed free.

So was Mary Magdalene. She was first to see the resurrected Jesus on resurrection morning. But long before then, Jesus had exorcized her of seven demons (Luke 8:1–4, John 20:1–18).

Two thousand years later, Beth, a junior in college in Ghana, claimed she had seventy demons. Two local Christian exorcists and four medical doctors failed to help her. She ended up in a hospital room defying sedation and decency. Alice, a mutual friend, took me to see Beth.

Goose pimpled as we entered Beth's room, I knew. There was nothing anyone could do. Give up on her. Or tune in to catch a giveaway. Would we wait forever? Not really. I prayed in silence, waiting and watching with all my antennas up. Forty-five minutes later I felt five pinpricks in my right-hand.

That's it, I said to myself, *five demons not seventy. Go for it. What if—? Never mind.* "You five demons," I said. "Leave Beth's body in Jesus' name."

An angry voice bellowed, "How do you know we're five? Here's home. We aren't going anywhere."

I shunned talking with this entity and I repeated the "out" order. At once, the bed rocked and started levitating. That scared Alice, Beth's nurses, and me. Everyone looked at me in terror, demanding answers. I looked at them in shock, clueless about the next step. The levitation went on for fifteen minutes and stopped. The resulting calm left Beth free.

Healing

Then there was a woman who suffered hemorrhage for twelve years. She touched the hem of Jesus' gown. And instantly the hemorrhage stopped (Mark 5:24–34).

Pat, a high school senior, didn't tell me how long she'd had painful menstruation when she asked me to pray for her. I'd just talked to the Christian club in her school in Accra, Ghana.

"I will," I said. Respecting her sensitivity about the subject, I hesitated. Although I didn't know what to pray, as I left her I began to pray.

Six months later Pat and I met again. She was all smiles. She said, "It's gone, thanks."

"You're welcome," I said, amazed.

Another example of healing took place in Jesus' life similarly (Matthew 8:1–4). A leper met Jesus and said to him, "If you are willing you can make me clean."

Jesus touched him and said, "I will, be clean."

And he was, just like that.

Harry wasn't a leper. But a sickness that nearly killed him at five forced his parents to migrate from Europe to the USA in search of an American medical marvel. Harry remained unwell for twenty-five years. His body rotted alive, retaining impressions like a ball of peanut butter.

I learned all this from Harry himself at Fuller Seminary in Pasadena, California. When he said, "The grapevine led me to you. Please pray for me."

"Don't believe everything you hear," I said. "I'm not a healer."

"I know," Harry said. "But please try."

That sucked me into his pain, filling my eyes with tears. I proposed the only way I knew. "Can you fast and pray with me for a miracle?"

"I wish. But my health can't afford it." His looks said it better and louder.

I fasted for thirty days and prayed for him by myself. On the thirty-first day, Harry and I prayed together. Three weeks later, Harry's doctor confirmed his inexplicable healing. Within three months, Harry regained hair that he'd lost chemo-fashion.

Conversion

It must have stunned Zacchaeus when Jesus said to him, "Zacchaeus, climb down. (Zacchaeus was a short man. He'd climbed a tree to see Jesus unhindered by the crowd.) I must stay in your house today" (Luke 19:1–10). A chief tax collector, a social reject, would host Jesus—how flattering to Zacchaeus.

While at dinner, Zacchaeus got up before Jesus and his disciples and fellow tax collectors he'd invited to meet Jesus. He said to Jesus, "Lord, I will give half my income to the poor. And I will pay back four times people I've cheated."

"Today salvation has come to this house," Jesus said.

Eager to bridge people to that experience, I ran a weekly evangelistic Bible study in a girls' boarding school while I was in the university in Kumasi, Ghana.

"I got to know Jesus personally at the first of those meetings," Agnes, a medical doctor living in Philadelphia, Pennsylvania, told me when she and I reconnected recently.

A heart encounter with Jesus is always life-changing. Jesus met a Samaritan woman at Jacob's well in Sychar and asked her for a drink of water (John 4:1–42).

"How can you, a Jew, ask me for a drink of water?" the woman protested because a Jew wouldn't drink from a cup a Samaritan had drunk from. But she and Jesus chatted about

Samaritan and Jewish cultures, temple and mountain religions, and preferred lifestyles. The woman raised all the issues.

She must have been impressed by this male Jew who defied social taboos to chat with her. But she wasn't convinced about everything he said. So she said, "I know that Messiah is coming. When he comes he'll tell us who's right and who's wrong on the issues."

Jesus stared at her and said, "I who speak with you am he."

In amazement, the woman left her water jar at the well. She ran to invite her townspeople to Jesus. After listening to Jesus, they said to her, "At first we believed because of your testimony. But after hearing Jesus ourselves, we know. He is indeed the Savior of the world."

Like Jesus, I walked in an unfamiliar neighborhood in Ghana, singing "The Old Rugged Cross" to myself, I thought.

A lady called from behind me, "Young man, please come here."

I went, wondering what I'd done.

"Hi, my name is Kate," she said and shook hands.

"I'm Wilson."

"Do you have a minute?" Kate asked.

"Sure," I said, my heart pounding.

We entered her house and sat in the living room.

"Please, sing for me the song you sang when I called you," Kate said.

I sang it.

"Sing it again, please."

I did. A third and fourth time, and I did.

"I'm a pastor's wife," Kate said, sobbing. "But I belong to a secret society. I threatened divorce the last time my husband and I quarreled about it two weeks ago. Your song convicted me to quit the secret society and get right with Jesus. Thanks for singing it for me."

"You're welcome," I said, utterly amazed.

These miracles surprised me. How they paralleled some of Jesus' miracles also surprised me, particularly because Jesus was deliberate and conscious about what he did. I, on the other hand, bumped into situations that could only be resolved through divine intervention. I might even walk past these people, not seeing them at all.

In hindsight, each of those miracles derived from a cluster of life-forming principles. The principles also paralleled Jesus' experience, which also surprised me. They are:

- dumb prayers
- reckless love
- foolish trust
- happy birthday
- ridiculous crawling
- tugs and nudges
- gushing life

How ordinary and yet, how profound. Together these life-forming principles scream, "Take the lid off the family likeness. Let it speak for itself." Why? God, who is outrageous love and loves outrageously, could only have kids who take after him. They in turn, love recklessly.

When ordinary folks know these life-forming principles and live by them as Jesus did, they unleash power that

- connects people to kingdom freedom and joy
- energizes the faith of many people
- matures those who are freed and energized into Jesus-likeness, to God's glory.

That's what *Family Likeness* is all about—those of us who follow Jesus should bear a resemblance to him and his thoughts and behavior. We should bear his likeness since we are in his family. This book is an invitation to take "like God, like people" as seriously as God does and watch what happens.

Section One: Dumb Prayers

CHAPTER 1

When God Prays Unembarrassed

To whom does God pray when he prays? Actually the Bible doesn't say God in three persons prays. It shows us Jesus, God in human form, who prayed.

For example, he prayed to multiply bread and fish to feed five thousand (John 6:1–14) and four thousand men (Matt. 15:29–39), not counting women and children. He prayed to raise Lazarus from the grave after he'd been buried four days (John 11:38–44). Many times he prayed all night long (Luke 6:12–16). He also prayed at dawn (Mark 1:35).

While it's inexplicable that Jesus, God in human form, should pray at all, Hebrews 5:7 says he even prayed to stay alive. "In the days of his flesh, Jesus offered up prayers and supplications, with loud cries and tears, to him who was able to save him from death, and he was heard for his godly fear."

Gethsemane is a snapshot of Jesus praying to be rescued from imminent death. He agonized so much he sweated blood. But God didn't rescue Jesus from death that time (Matt. 26:36–46). Where are those times when Jesus prayed to be rescued from death, and the Father did?

Joseph and Mary's escape to Egypt with the baby Jesus saved Jesus from Herod's sword. But it wasn't the baby Jesus who prayed to be rescued from death. Neither was it Mary and Joseph. They didn't know death was about to snatch the baby Jesus.

It was God the Father, who knew about it and ordered and orchestrated the rescue (Matt. 2:1–23). But that incident began a death chase for Jesus. Death attacks on Jesus popped up like land mines right from the beginning of his public ministry.

First, in the synagogue at Nazareth, Jesus read his job description from Isaiah 61:1–2.

> The Spirit of the Lord is upon me, because he has anointed me to preach good news to the poor. He has sent me to proclaim release to the captives and recovery of sight to the blind, to set at liberty those who are oppressed, to proclaim the acceptable year of the Lord.
>
> (Luke 4:18–19)

That outraged all those in the synagogue (Luke 4:16–30). They jostled Jesus to the edge of a cliff to push him over. But Jesus slipped through their hands and was gone. What a narrow escape.

The second incident occurred in the temple. Leading priests and Pharisees rushed on Jesus to stone him to death for saying, "Before Abraham was, I am" (John 7:53–8:59). But Jesus hid himself and went out of the temple, another just-in-time escape from death.

A third time, the supreme religious council of Israel and the Pharisees cried out, "Blasphemy, blasphemy." They swooped on Jesus to tear him to pieces for saying, "I and the Father are one" (John 10:31–39). But again, the Father rescued him just in time.

Fourth, the supreme religious council of Israel and the Pharisees asked Jesus, "Show us your resume" (Matt. 21:23–46). Instead, Jesus told them stories about God's mercy to merciless managers. They saw themselves in those stories. Outraged, they became thugs and rushed on Jesus as a mob to kill him. Mysteriously, again God rescued Jesus.

Fifth, theologian bureaucrats confronted Jesus about Jews paying taxes to Caesar. Whether he answered yes or no, Jesus wouldn't win. That way they'd trap him in his own words, arrest him, and turn him over to Roman authorities (Matt. 22:15–46).

But Jesus outwitted them. "Give to Caesar what belongs to him. And give to God what belongs to him," he said. Narrowly, Jesus escaped premature death again.

The sixth time, Satan entered Judas to betray Jesus to the Pharisees (Luke 22:1–6). While Judas led soldiers and guards to arrest Jesus, Jesus prayed with loud cries and tears (Luke 22:39–46, compare Matt. 26:36–46). This time, the Father didn't rescue him.

The first five instances must be some of those times when the Father rescued Jesus from the jaws of premature death. But the suddenness of the attacks gave Jesus no time to pray. Therefore most likely, Jesus must have foreseen them and prayed about them. The result was that the Father rescued him from unnecessary death. And the basis, according to the Hebrews passage, was Jesus' godly fear (Heb. 5:7).

Why didn't the Father rescue him just because God's agenda and reputation were at stake? Why not because Jesus was (and is) God? All that aside, why must Jesus (God) pray before God the Father saved his own agenda from being terminated in premature death. An unnecessary death?

If Jesus died a premature death, he wouldn't reach the point when Judas, Satan, the Sanhedrin, Herod, Pilate, and Rome would unite to fight God (Luke 22:1–6, John 18–19, Acts 4:23–28, compare Gen. 3:15 and Ps. 2:1–2). The crucifixion wouldn't be the place where Jesus would make himself human God-defiance (sin) for God to punish him as sin deserves.

Why didn't the Father snatch his own purpose from wreckage? He's God. He could. Or why didn't Jesus coast along, taking it easy, bluffing his way through it all as the all-powerful God, albeit in human form?

But as God in human form, he prayed unembarrassed. Why? And unembarrassed, God the Father rescued him from death on the basis of Jesus' godly fear.

Jesus demonstrated the same godly fear at Gethsemane as well. Three times he prayed, saying, "My Father, if it is possible, may this cup be taken from me. Yet not as I will, but as you will" (Matt. 26:39, 42 and 44). But the Father didn't rescue him this time. Jesus suffered the brutalities of the cross (John 18–19).

He suffered God's wrath for human God-defiance or sin (Matt. 27:45–46, compare Isa. 53). And yet, the last thing Jesus did before he died was to pray again. "Father, into your hands I commit my spirit" (Luke 23:46). Did he have to pray for that too?

Enthroned above all rule and authority and power and dominion (Luke 22:29, Eph. 1:18–23), Jesus continues to pray. This time the Holy Spirit, also God, joins him. God and God pray to God, unembarrassed.

It would make some human sense if those prayers were directed at human and spiritual God-defiance, which though defeated hasn't conceded defeat. An outraged Satan would only intensify the rule of satanic principles of defiance, force, greed, selfishness, and evil ambition to resist losing victims to Jesus.

But according to Romans 8:26–27 and 34 and Hebrews 7:25, Jesus and the Holy Spirit pray no such prayers. Rather, they pray for the saints. Why? To suggest that those prayers beg God to accept the saints contradicts the semantics. The saints are the saved and sanctified, repentant people.

It's worse to suggest that God requires the prayers of Jesus and the Spirit as an addition to Jesus' death. Jesus had said he'd paid it all. "It's finished [accomplished]," before he died (John 19:30). About seven hundred years before Jesus came, Isaiah had said that Jesus' death would be it—no additions needed (Isa. 53:10–12).

So why are Jesus and the Holy Spirit praying for the saints? The scriptures don't tell us. But they're full of God's responses to prayers of saints who prayed, like Jesus and the Holy Spirit, when it made no sense to pray. David and Paul are typical.

CHAPTER 2

When People Pray Dumb Prayers

Surprise, surprise, a thousand years before Jesus, David prayed like Jesus. David didn't have to pray in the context he did. God made him king while Saul wore the crown and sat on the throne. Certainly, God must have a solution for the problem he'd created for David.

But as far as we know, God didn't tell David about it. What we know is that David ran while he prayed and prayed running from King Saul, who sought to kill him. A death chase stalked David as it would Jesus.

David killed Goliath, Israel's archenemy, and won a great victory for King Saul (1 Sam. 17:41–54). But he got into trouble. The lyrics of the women's song credited David with ten thousands while crediting Saul with thousands, a statement of fact (1 Sam. 18:7–9). But Saul wouldn't have it. He set out to kill David for it.

Twice, Saul tried to pin David to the wall with his spear while David lured an evil spirit away from Saul with his harp. Saul failed (1 Sam. 16:11–23, 18:10–11, 19:8–10). David married Michal, Saul's daughter, not knowing that Saul planned to exploit the marriage and kill him in his sleep. Michal helped David escape (1 Sam. 19:11–17).

David sought sanctuary with Samuel. Saul sent three batches of assassins after David, joining the fourth group himself. But the Spirit of God paralyzed all four batches. Including Saul, would-be assassins dropped their swords and prophesied instead (1 Sam. 19:17–24).

From there David ran to a nearby "seminary." Saul chased him there. He barely missed killing him, instead he killed eighty-five students and their professors for giving sanctuary to David, the king's number one enemy (1 Sam. 22:11–23). But for a Philistine invasion that pulled King Saul back home, he would have killed David in the desert of Maon (1 Sam. 23:24–29).

Even so, Saul blocked David from the throne. Reaching it and the crown remained humanly impossible. Why didn't David coast along, complacent because God made him king? He'd reach the throne and crown laidback.

On the other hand, why didn't he blame God when King Saul hunted him in caves and deserts to kill him? (See 1 Sam. 22:1–2, 23:13, 25:13). How come, like Jesus, he prayed revering God and depending on God to rescue him when and how he saw fit (see Ps. 22–41, 55–64, compare 2 Sam. 22)?

And like Jesus, ahead of Jesus, David didn't avenge himself. Twice he found King Saul unguarded. But because he feared God, he didn't kill him (see 1 Samuel 24 and 26). He even mourned when Saul died in battle (see 2 Sam. 1, compare 2:8–10, 3:22–39, 4:5–11, 5:8).

After Saul's death David didn't take the crown and throne. He ruled only Judah that had accepted him as their king. Seven years he waited. Then Israel too accepted him as their king (2 Sam. 5).

In David, the fear of God, intimacy with God, passion for God's glory, radical obedience to God and his Word, and integrity, blended into a lifestyle of prayer and worship, trust, and dependence on God (see Ps. 119, 138–150, compare 1 Sam. 16:12–23, 18:12–16, 23:1–5, 30:8, 2 Sam. 2:1, 5:19, and 23).

That was David in Jesus' likeness a thousand years before Jesus came. But five years after Jesus' resurrection and ascension, Paul behaved similarly. Again, it was as if Jesus put Paul in harm's way when he made him an apostle. A death chase for him began in Damascus.

Jews in Damascus felt betrayed by Paul. He arrived, advocating the Jesus he'd hated. They plotted to kill Paul. The plot leaked out. A basket flight over the city wall at night sneaked Paul out to Jerusalem (Acts 9:1–25).

But Jerusalem also proved hostile for Paul. On the one hand, the apostles and disciples believed Paul's conversion to Jesus only after Barnabas' mediation. The Hellenist Jews, on the other hand, quickly noticed Paul's defection to Jesus. They resented it and sought to kill Paul for it. Paul ran again, this time to Tarsus, his hometown, forsaken (Acts 9:26–30).

Eight years crawled by. Then Barnabas showed up in Tarsus and invited Paul to Antioch. Together, they taught for a year at the First International Church of Antioch (Acts 11:19–26). From there, the Holy Spirit sent Barnabas and Paul out as apostles to non-Jews (Acts 13:1–3).

Elymas, a Jewish occultist, resisted them at Paphos, Cyprus, their first stop. With occult power, he blocked Sergius Paulus, a Roman governor, from converting to faith in Jesus. Paul blinded Elymas. The effect broke the occult power and spell and freed Sergius Paulus to understand the gospel and convert to faith in Jesus (Acts 13:4–12).

Another Jewish resistance forced Barnabas and Paul out of Antioch, Pisidia (Acts 13:45, 50). They escaped stoning at Iconium (Acts 14:1–7).

But Jews from Antioch and Iconium chased Barnabas and Paul to Lystra. They poisoned the minds of citizenry and stoned Paul, who survived. The next day he and Barnabas resumed their travels and, retracing their steps, they strengthened the believers, telling them, "Through [much suffering] we must enter the kingdom of God" (Acts 14:8–22). And they moved on.

At Philippi, Paul freed a slave girl from a divination spirit. That put Paul and Silas in jail. Their jail time led to the conversion of the jailer and his family (Acts 16:11–34). But persistent, Asian Jews chased Paul to Jerusalem.

They stirred Jerusalem mobs against him and tried to mob-kill him. A Roman tribune rescued him just in time (Acts 21:27–26:32). The temple arrest evolved into a jail sentence in Caesarea and house arrest in Rome (Acts 27–28).

Like Jesus and David, Paul didn't coast along to get there. Rather, he prayed, revering God and depending on him to rescue him when and how he saw fit. He asked other believers to pray for him (Rom. 16:30, Eph. 6:18–20, compare Acts 4:23–31).

These other instances of the role that what seemed to be foolish fasting and prayer played (or could play) are well known:

- In Ezekiel 22:30–31, God disclosed to Ezekiel that he had let Babylon conquer and exile Judah, as punishment for their idolatry because he found no one to intercede for Judah (compare Gen. 18:16–19:29).

- In Daniel 10, Daniel fasted and prayed not knowing why, and God sent an angelic reinforcement to break a three-week evil spirit hold-off to release an angel God had earlier sent to him.
- In Esther 4–10, Queen Esther, Mordecai, and others' fasting and prayer crashed a set-in-stone Persian imperial decree to annihilate the Jews and preserved the promise and hope of the birth of Jesus, about four hundred years before he was born.
- In Nehemiah 1, it was senseless for Nehemiah, King Xerxes' cupbearer, to fast and pray after the seventy years of Judah's exile had ended. But the result was that King Xerxes authorized and funded the rebuilding of the walls of Jerusalem under Nehemiah's leadership (compare Neh. 2–13 and Jer. 25:11–12, 29:1–14).
- In Matthew 9:35–38, Jesus asked his disciples to pray that God would send workers into his own vineyard.
- In Matthew 26:38, Jesus, God in human form, asked Peter, James, and John to pray for him just before his arrest (compare John 18:1–14 and Matt. 26:69–75).

This list needn't be exhaustive to say what it says. God prayed and continues to pray unembarrassed. Unashamed, God asked and still asks for prayer. And just as he'd answered what seemed to be "dumb" prayers, praying when it made no sense to pray, he does so today. His invitations to pray dumb prayers come through jolts of

- compassion, not pity
- righteous outrage, not condemnation
- impossible personal need, not want

A Jolt of Compassion, not Pity

Dell and I barely knew each other in Colorado Springs, where he worked with a Christian organization. He took me to lunch on a Wednesday. While we waited for our food, he said, avoiding eye contact, "Can you pray for me without knowing the issue?"

I thought, *Perhaps Dell is embarrassed to tell me his problem.* He was old enough to be my dad. So I said, "I guess."

"I've had it for a long, long time." Dell's voice cracked and he soaked tears from his eyes with a paper napkin. He hung his head and said, "Just pray for me, okay?"

By now I'd entered his pain neck-deep. But I didn't feel ready to pray. So I said, "Dell, can I fast tomorrow then we pray the next day?" How dumb.

"Sure," he said and raised his head, looking somewhat disappointed.

We met in the same restaurant two days later and prayed. A week later he reported two deliverances from the same problem, his and his son's. Amazingly, he hadn't said his son also had the unnamed problem. Moreover, the son was away in Mexico at the time of prayer. But most amazing, when they compared notes, Dell realized he and his son were released at the time he and I prayed. What a God.

A Jolt of Righteous Outrage, not Condemnation

While in high school in Ghana, I discovered that most high schools demanded attendance at Sunday morning or evening worship services. But they didn't make the worship services relevant or meaningful to students.

The irrelevant and meaningless religious rites disgruntled many students, making them hate church and God. School authorities seemed uncaring. The situation saddened and distressed me. It drove me into fasting and praying, "Lord God, please do something about this situation." How dumb. Yet somehow, I kept at it for seven months.

In the eighth, I met the Reverend Peter Barker, a British missionary to Ghana, in a bookstore. He asked me how I was. I read genuineness in his eyes, so I told him about my pain and prayer.

He connected me with a fraternity of pastors in Accra that dated back to the 1800s. The fraternity accepted blame, explaining that pastors got busier and busier in churches and had no time left for worship services in schools. But pastors' busyness hadn't changed.

The fraternity decided to form an Accra Chaplaincy Board (ACB), made up of non-clergy, to include me, to take care of that need. Since its formation, ACB has sent an average of fifty preachers weekly to the schools in Accra and its suburbs.

Volunteer preachers came from among missionaries, Christian faculty in local schools, and Christian college graduates resident in Accra. In five years, ACB rippled throughout major cities in Ghana.

A Jolt of an Impossible Personal Need, not a Want

Six years ago, I developed a sinus problem that exhausted all known medical treatment for sinus infections. A frustrated medical doctor walked me through the result of a blood test he'd ordered.

It declared me allergic, not only to pollen and dust, dogs and cats, and heat and cold. I was also allergic to green and dried leaves, gasoline and perfume, stores and restaurants, and trapped cooking smells and recycled air on planes. What I heard in what he said was this: The only place I could live free from allergies was outside this world.

"I'm sorry," the doctor finally said. "There's nothing else we can do for you." He issued a refill for an old prescription.

On my way home I thought about the new reality I had to live with. I think I prayed, but I don't recall what I said. As I pulled to a halt at a stop sign, the name Hezekiah came to mind. *Hezekiah*, I thought. *What has he got to do with it?*

Back home I located Hezekiah in 2 Kings 18–19. I read and reread the story. Suddenly, certain parallels formed in my mind.

I saw myself as Hezekiah, my sinus problem as King Sennacherib of Assyria, his letter to King Hezekiah as my latest blood test result, and total extinction of Israel as the defiance of my allergic condition. Could I do what King Hezekiah did?

King Hezekiah took King Sennacherib's letter and spread it on the altar before God, admitting his helplessness against Assyria, the world power of the day. He prayed that God would do something to let King Sennacherib know that he'd crossed the line. In bragging that nothing, not even God, could rescue any nation from his hand, King Sennacherib had exalted himself above his Creator, the Lord God.

Certainly, the allergist didn't go that far when he told me I'd come to the end of what medical science could do to help me. But King Hezekiah's action screamed, "Cry to God as I did." Could I? Should I?

The implications looked weird, insane. But I pulled out my copy of the blood test result and spread it out on my desk. With a juicy red marker and a ruler, I drew two parallel lines diagonally across it. Between the lines, an inch apart, I wrote 2 Kings 19:1–37. And I prayed, "Lord, please do something." Next, I emptied the medicine cabinet of all the allergy medications and prescriptions and tossed them into the trash can. "This is it," I said.

And indeed, that was it. Gone, the defiant allergies ran. How amazing. The amazement speaks to the point. Dumb prayers are a trait of family likeness with the God who prays unembarrassed. How might reckless love and foolish trust show that likeness?

SECTION TWO: RECKLESS LOVE

CHAPTER 3

When God Loves Outrageously

Wat do you do with a God who catches up with you at the place where your rebellion against him and desertion of him had crashed, and he says, "Kid, are you hurt?"

David was typical. Here was the friend of God. God had called him "a man after my heart" while he was still a youth. But King David took Bathsheba, the wife of Uriah, a captain in David's army, while Uriah was away in battle. David kept Bathsheba in his embrace and had Uriah killed in cold blood. And he hid his acts, not knowing, while they festered they cried to God like Abel's blood at Cain's hand (compare Gen. 4:10).

When prophet Nathan confronted David about it, he admitted he'd sinned. That was when he wrote Psalm 51, one of the most eloquent prayers of confession ever written. Swiftly, God said, "I also forgive you." How could he? (see story in 2 Sam. 11–12).

True, multiple incest, coups, sibling murders, political unrest, and more followed in David's life from that time on (2 Sam. 13–24). But David remained

- the man after God's heart, and
- the ancestor of Jesus through Solomon, the son of David and Bathsheba.

And forever, Jesus is called "the son of David." If that isn't outrageous love, what is?

Another example was Paul. Paul was an elite theologian turned thuggish. He'd witnessed the death of Stephen. After that, he dragged children and women and men from bed and from dinner. He lined them up to be stoned to death. Their crime was that they defected from the lifeless code of ethics that the Sanhedrin policed to Jesus—the way, the truth and the life (John 14:6).

As a commissioned devotee of that code, Paul went to Damascus to arrest the followers of Jesus and bring them to Jerusalem, to be charged for defection and killed. On the road, Jesus appeared to him in a blinding light. Dazed by the light, Paul's horse tossed him off, and he thudded to the ground like a sack of potatoes.

"Saul, Saul," Jesus called (Saul was his name at the time). "Why do you persecute me?"

It was as if Jesus said to him, "Kid, are you hurt?"

Instantly, Paul acknowledged Jesus as Lord (Acts 9).

And at once Jesus made Paul his apostle to non-Jews. Paul preached Jesus as Lord from Jerusalem to Europe, planting churches and mentoring Timothy, Luke, Titus, and many others (Rom. 16:18–19). He also wrote thirteen of the twenty-seven books of the New Testament. Like David after Bathsheba, Paul remains a product of God's outrageous love.

Jesus showed outrageous love to social rejects similarly. Jewish society of Jesus' day confined lepers to outlying wastelands. When Jesus bumped into them, he touched them and healed them. Jesus hung out with prostitutes and tax collectors while society scorned them, treating them as social rejects, comparable to AIDS patients today.

Then, contrary to contemporary Jewish practice, Jesus spent two nights in Sychar, a town in Samaria, converting and discipling Samaritans. And while priests avoided a corpse like the plague, Jesus touched corpses and gave them life. On top of that, Jesus loved sinners, the socially correct and social rejects alike. He died like a criminal to save them, having said, "Greater love has no man than this, that a man lay down his life for his friends" (John 15:13).

Why would the sinless one call sinners his friends? (1 John 3:16). But that's the nature of outrageous love. His enemies, the Pharisees, couldn't miss it. They nicknamed Jesus the friend of sinners to discredit him. Not knowing, they confirmed the fact that indeed Jesus is the friend of sinners (Luke 5:29–32, Matt. 11:19, compare Luke 7:33–35).

God's love is not only outrageous; it's sufficient, selfless, and sacrificial. It's joy, peace, patience, kindness, goodness, faithfulness, gentleness, and self-control. It's the fruit of the Spirit (Gal. 5:22–23, compare the wisdom of God, James 3:17).

People may try. But they can't produce outrageous love. They have an inherited proneness and an acquired proneness that inhibit them. The inherited proneness is thought and behavioral patterns that grow out of defiance, force, greed, selfishness, and evil ambition. These are satanic principles that Eve and Adam accessed and passed on to humanity after them.

The acquired proneness is a repackage of the legacy. It's a post-conversion unwillingness to let God, God's Word, or

God's Spirit have the last word on good and bad, right and wrong, and true and false. That's why only the Holy Spirit can produce outrageous love (Gal. 5:22–23).

In principle, as believers in Jesus, we have the Spirit as proof that we belong to Jesus (Rom. 8:9). That's not enough. We're to be led moment by moment by the Spirit (Rom. 8:14). In addition, we are to be being filled, controlled and empowered by the Spirit (Eph. 5:18).

The reality becomes a way of life, when

- we don't lie to the Spirit, and we aren't hypocritical (Acts 5:3)
- we don't abuse the Spirit, and we don't take his mercy for granted (Acts 5:9)
- we don't resist the Spirit, and we don't find excuses to disobey his cues, tugs, and nudges (Acts 7:51)
- we don't grieve the Spirit, and we don't justify unforgiveness or revenge (Eph. 4:30)
- we don't quench the Spirit, and we don't settle for living in the natural, insisting on interpreting all things from purely human perspectives (1 Thess. 5:19).

That's the context in which the Spirit produces outrageous love in believers in Jesus. In Paul's words, God's outrageous love becomes reckless love when produced in people. Expressed, it's patient and kind. Therefore it's not proud, rude, self-seeking, or easily angered. Consequently, it doesn't envy, boast, keep a record of wrongs, delight in evil, or end. Rather, it always rejoices with the truth, protects, trusts, hopes, and perseveres (1 Cor. 13:4–8).

But just like Jesus doesn't impose being saved on us, the Spirit doesn't impose his fruit of love on us. Yet it's only reckless love for people and foolish trust in God that discern when to pray dumb prayers, and continue praying when it doesn't seem sensible.

In short, dumb prayers are impossible without reckless love and foolish trust.

CHAPTER 4

When People Love Recklessly

You may recall Harry from the Introduction to this book. Harry died slowly for twenty-five years. His body rotted alive, defying the best medical treatment money could buy. But prayer ended the slow dying and decaying process just like that.

Harry recovered not only health, but life and a robust and firm body. Hair that he'd lost chemo-fashion in the past twenty-five years grew back full in three months.

What made the difference wasn't just prayer. It was prayer bathed in reckless love. Recklessly, I gave Harry not a week but a month of my life, fasting and praying for him. Harry could never pay me enough for that. That's the nature of love.

Jesus loved Harry and me outrageously. I turned around and loved Harry recklessly. Galatians 6:9–10 says, "Let us not grow weary in well-doing. . . . So then, as we have opportunity, let us do good to all men, and especially to those who are of the household of faith." Harry and I and Laurel (see below) are siblings in that household.

I had met Harry in grad school in Pasadena, California. Then I met Laurel at Mission Training International (MTI) in Colorado Springs. She and I were part of a team of six that trained outbound missionaries in two- to five-week training programs. Unlike the rest of us on the team, Laurel was single. She'd never married.

One day she and I rode to Pinecrest Lodge, the training site at Pleasant, Colorado. She drove. Halfway along the trip, I asked her, "Laurel, do you want to be married?"

"What kind of question is that?" she asked, chuckling.

"You know what I mean. Do you want a husband?"

"Do you have someone eligible?"

"No."

"Then why do you ask?"

"I'm thinking," I said. "If you really, really want to, I'll agree with you to pray that you get a husband."

"Are you kidding?"

"How could I?"

"Bless you, dear," she said.

Starting that morning, I prayed every day for Laurel to get not just a husband. Sometimes I fasted when there didn't seem a need for it and prayed for someone who'd sweep her off her feet. A year later, she and I stopped working for MTI. She went to work with Greater Europe mission there in Colorado Springs. I went to Mission Moving Mountains in Minneapolis, Minnesota and continued praying, "dumb," prayers for Laurel.

Ten months later, the phone rang. "Hi, it's me, Laurel."

After we'd chitchatted, Laurel said, "Are you sitting down?"

"What are you up to? No."

"Please sit down."

I did.

"I'm getting married!" Laurel said and laughed the heartiest I've ever heard her.

"Congratulations!" I screamed, ecstatic.

"Know what?"

"What?"

"I want you to walk me down the aisle."

When Laurel was a missionary school principal in Zambia, I was in fifth grade in Ghana. Now I'm to play a father's role at her wedding? How flattering.

"You mean that?" I asked, overwhelmed.

"You bet."

Reckless love, piped through dumb prayers, comes full circle, doesn't it?

Six months before I started praying for Laurel, she had coordinated a three-week pre-field orientation program. She, Tom, and I taught in it. It had twenty-three outbound missionaries participating. Among them was Robert, a medical doctor who was going to Pakistan.

After the last session on Friday the second week, while Laurel and Tom headed for the van, Robert took me aside and said, "I wish I knew the joy of leading at least one person to believe in Jesus before going on missions. I'll be gone in six months."

Robert's face reddened. He looked away and wiped tears from his eyes with both hands. "I'm sorry," he said when he turned to face me.

"No problem," I said. "But, tell me, Robert. Why is that important for you?"

"I know in principle that all Christians should tell others about Jesus," he said. "The conversion stories you tell in class show it's doable. But I've never had the experience. I want to. Please help me." Robert sounded and looked desperate.

We were now outside the building. Tom had honked, it was time to go. Judgmental love shouted. How come Robert's mission agency didn't address the issue while recruiting him? Were they setting him up to fail? With one week left of the pre-field orientation, what extra help could I give even if I wanted to?

Besides, I was battling a cold that left me exhausted. I looked forward to relaxing that weekend to recover and get ready for the last week of the three-week program. *Too bad, Robert, that's your problem. Go fix it. And leave me alone.*

Quickly, reckless love objected. Remember, reckless love, like God's outrageous love, is sufficient, selfless, and sacrificial.

"Yes, yes," I said in agreement. Before I hopped on the van, I said, "Robert, I'll fast and pray for you about it this weekend."

I did.

Monday morning Robert met Laurel, Tom, and me at the door to the lodge. He was all smiles.

"Wilson, Wilson," he called, ecstatic. "It happened."

"It did?"

"Yes."

Laurel and Tom walked on to the basement classroom where a piano rendering of "Fairest Lord Jesus" said it was time for group devotions. Robert and I stood aside in the lobby. And he said, "Half past eleven o'clock Saturday night, I was in the lobby all alone, catching up on the newspapers. In came a husband and wife to check in for bed-n-breakfast. They went upstairs to locate their room."

"And," I said.

"The man returned to the lobby. He and I chitchatted for a while. Before we knew it, we were talking about life after death. I shared my hope in Jesus with him."

"I need such confidence," the man said. "Tell me how."

"I told him," Robert said. "And he prayed to give his life to Jesus. It was now two o'clock in the morning. We exchanged business cards and said good night. At ten o'clock Sunday morning, he and his wife checked out."

Robert danced around and hugged me, saying, "It's amazing. Now I too have a conversion story to tell. I can hardly keep it down."

"I'm happy for you, Robert," I said. "Congratulations."

"Thanks for praying for me," he said. "I know you did. My fears about witnessing for Jesus are gone, gone forever."

Robert's freedom and empowerment came through "dumb" fasting and praying steeped in reckless love. The Holy Spirit anticipated that when he said,

> If anyone says, "I love God," and hates [cares nothing for] his brother, he is a liar; for he who does not love his brother whom he has seen, cannot love God whom he has not seen. . . . He who loves God should love his brother also.
>
> (1 John 4:20–21)

Jesus, after quoting God the Father, "You shall love the Lord your God with all your heart, and with all your soul, and with all your mind, and with all your strength" (Mark 12:30, compare Deut. 6:4–5), added

> A new commandment I give to you, that you love one another; even as I have loved you, that you also love one another. By this all men will know that you are my disciples, if you have love for one another.
>
> (John 13:34–35)

Jesus was confident we would love one another. So he asked us to also love people who treat us like dirt.

> But I say to you, "Love your enemies and pray for those who persecute you, so that you may be sons of your Father who is

in heaven; for he makes his sun rise on the evil and the good, and sends rain on the just and on the unjust."

(Matt. 5:44–45)

Typical of Jesus, he modeled what he wants us to do. Just before he died, he prayed for Caiaphas, the Pharisees, Herod, Pilate, and the soldiers, who denied him justice, mocked him, and crucified him. "Father, forgive them; for they know not what they do" (Luke 23:34).

Put together, the Father, Jesus, and the Spirit are saying, "Take the lid off the family likeness. Let it speak for itself." Why? God, who is outrageous love and loves outrageously, could only have kids who take after him. They, in turn, love recklessly. How can the world resist recognizing the uniqueness of that love? (John 17:20–23). And because love is winsome and contagious, some might even seek God as they see his love in us.

But my reckless love for Robert, Laurel, and Harry would have resulted in nothing if it lacked the support of foolish trust in God to come through for them. It was the blend of foolish trust in God and reckless love that fueled and sustained my dumb prayers for them. How does that work?

SECTION THREE: FOOLISH TRUST

CHAPTER 5

When God Trusts, Betrayed

How can you do this to me?" Teresa said in the doorway to Tim's study, raging. She moved in closer to him.

Tim peeled off a handwritten note he was reading to look at her. "What are you talking about?" he said.

"Don't feign ignorance. Phyllis is carrying your baby."

Phyllis was sixteen. She was Teresa's sister, whom Teresa and Tim had raised from age six, four years before their only child, Vickie, arrived.

Tim got up to leave the room. Teresa pushed him back down, "Sit down. Are you out of your mind? You've wrecked our lives. Can't you see it?"

Tim rubbed his eyes. "What can I say?" he mumbled, avoiding eye contact. "What's done is done. Can we move on?"

"To what?" Teresa said and stormed out of the room.

In three weeks, Teresa moved out of Tim's life. Tim had lost his wife, a sweetheart from high school, forever. He'd broken trust. And that was it.

Incidentally, most people God trusted broke trust. For example, God trusted Adam. He included him in the creation process. He let Adam name the animals and birds—whatever Adam called them was their name (Gen. 2:19, 23).

Then God appointed Adam and Eve as rulers of the creation (Gen. 1:26–31). But Eve and Adam sold their rule, themselves, and humanity after them, three-for-a-penny, to Satan (Gen. 3:1–24, compare Luke 4:5–7, 1 John 5:19, Rev. 12:9). Yet God peopled the world through them, not by obligation or lack of options (Gen. 4–5). He could have accomplished this any way he chose, but he did it through Adam and Eve.

Similarly, God showed great trust when he chose Abraham to enter a self-revealing relationship with him. He promised Abraham a son and children as innumerable as the stars (Gen. 12–15). Abraham believed it and God counted it to him as righteousness (Gen. 15:6).

One day, Sarah took Abraham for a walk.

"Tell me, my lord," she said. "Did God tell you how you and I were to have the son he promised?"

Sarah implied that Abraham knew that she was seventy-five and barren. She wanted to know if Abraham left out something when he told her what God said.

"Hmm, let me think," Abraham said. "No."

"That's what I thought," Sarah said.

A boulder offered a lovers' seat. They sat on it, facing the sunset. Sarah fondly tugged Abraham's beard.

"Listen to me, my lord. Look at my maid, Hagar. She's young and pretty. I'll bring her to your bed. You know the custom.

Since it's I who give her to you, she'll deliver her kid on my knees, making the kid mine."

Abraham sighed and looked at Sarah. "Sarah, that's culturally correct. But don't you think we're being presumptuous when God hasn't given us directions about this yet?"

"Why would he?" Sarah said and got up, her gaze glued to the setting sun. "You don't expect God to tell us what we know, do you?"

Abraham hung his head, deep in thought.

Sarah continued, "I'm going back. Are you coming?" She glanced at him and started walking away.

"Sure," Abraham said. He got up and followed her.

They walked in silence. But just before they reached the camp, Sarah said, "My lord, you must know that your no in this matter denies me a wife's right. But if that's what you want, fine. You're the righteous one. You hear God. The rest of us don't. Your will be done."

"No, my love," Abraham said and stepped ahead of Sarah. He held her shoulders and stared into her eyes. He blinked and said half-smiling, "Your will rather be done."

A year later, Ishmael arrived (Gen. 16:1–16) and so did troubles Sarah couldn't anticipate or handle. She wanted Hagar and Ishmael out, and Ishmael and Hagar went out. But the problem stayed behind. Why?

The real problem was Sarah and Abraham's scheme. It resorted to a Near Eastern custom and eliminated the need to wait, trust, and depend on God to give them the promised son when and how he saw fit.

Abraham broke trust with God. Ripple effects would outlive Abraham. Yet God let Abraham and Sarah have Isaac. Abraham was now a hundred years old while Sarah was ninety (Gen. 17–26). Abraham remained the father of all who trust and depend on God alone to save them (Gen. 18:16–19, compare Gen. 15:6).

God trusted the descendants of Abraham when he rescued them in the exodus (Ex. 1–31). But they broke trust through the worship of golden calves (Gen. 32, 1 Kings 12, 2 Kings 21). Yet God entrusted them with the Old Testament Scriptures. And Jesus, God in human from, came to the world through them.

God's trust for David is also well known (see chapter 3). God made him king over all Israel while David was still a youth and while Saul reigned as king (1 Sam. 16–2 Sam. 10). God boasted of David as the man after his heart. But David broke trust. He took Bathsheba, Uriah's wife, and had Uriah killed in cold blood (2 Sam. 11–12).

Yet David remained the ancestor of Jesus. Jesus is named Son of David (Luke 1:32, compare Luke 1:26–56).

Did Jesus not trust Peter, James, and John similarly? He revealed himself especially to them at the mount of transfiguration (Matt. 16:13–17:8, compare 2 Pet. 1:16). Moments before his arrest, Jesus bared his heart only to these three, "My soul is very sorrowful even to death; remain here, and watch with me" (Matt. 26:37–38, compare John 18:1–14).

They slept instead. Not only that, they too abandoned Jesus at his arrest when the other apostles did. Shortly afterward, Peter swore he never knew Jesus (Matt. 26:69–75). Yet Jesus left Peter in charge of fellow believers. "I have prayed for you that your faith may not fail," Jesus told him. "When you have turned again, strengthen your brethren" (Luke 22:31–32).

Jesus didn't stop Peter from denying him. Rather, he prayed for him ahead of time that the denial might not shatter his faith. Confident about that, Jesus charged Peter to:

- nurture younger believers to maturity
- take care of the older ones to help them be productive
- feed both the older and younger people appropriately (John 21:22, compare Prov. 27:23).

Jesus' stubborn trust in Peter is right there, shouting, "Take charge, Peter." Why did Jesus trust Peter so much that he appointed him leader of his immediate followers?

Jesus knew that the Holy Spirit was coming. He would not only empower Peter (and the other apostles and disciples) to be credible and effective witnesses for Jesus (Luke 24:48–49, compare Acts 1:1–11). He'd also help Peter and the others recall how Jesus modeled childlike trust and dependence on God. They'd recall with fresh meaning those times when Jesus prayed and trusted the Father to rescue him from premature death, when and how he saw fit (Luke 4:28–30, John 8:48–59, John 10:31–49, compare Heb. 5:7–10).

Then the Spirit would remind them about Jesus' insistence that their authenticity and effectiveness come from depending on Jesus alone.

> I am the true vine, and my Father is the vinedresser . . .
> Abide in me, and I in you. As the branch cannot bear fruit
> by itself, unless it abides in the vine, neither can you, unless
> you abide in me. I am the vine, you are the branches. He
> who abides in me, and I in him, he it is that bears much
> fruit, for apart from me you can do nothing.
>   (John 15:1–5, compare Luke 10:1–9,
>   17–19, John 14:26, and Acts 1–14)

Neither would succeeding generations of believers in Jesus be authentic and effective without Jesus. Therefore the Spirit would remind them also about their need to trust and depend on God like a child (John 16:12–15). After all, childlike trust and dependence on God are the flip side of God's trust in people, even when they break trust.

CHAPTER 6

When People Trust Foolishly

It pops up everywhere in the Bible. Jesus and the Spirit agree that childlike trust and dependence on God are inevitable.

Jesus declared, "It's impossible to enter the kingdom of God without childlike trust and dependence on God" (Luke 18:17). Again he said, "Only childlike trust and dependence on God can see the transcendence of God" (John 11:40). Jesus told Martha just before he raised Lazarus from the grave.

Then through the author of Hebrews, the Spirit said no one can please, delight, or serve God acceptably without childlike trust and dependence on God (Heb. 11:6). What are childlike trust and dependence on God? And why are they so important?

Childlike trust and dependence on God are not skepticism, disbelief, unbelief, or faithlessness. Nudged or tugged, for example, to pray that twenty-year-old Alyssa would live when her doctor says she'd die of cancer in two months:

- victims of faithlessness hesitate, juggling "what-if" excuses
- victims of unbelief ask for more and more information
- victims of disbelief demand proof beyond reasonable doubt
- victims of skepticism turn the other way, cynical

Why? These responses grow out of satanic principles of defiance, force, greed, selfishness, and evil ambition. The latter began with Lucifer (now Satan, see Isaiah 14). People and spirits personalize them and live by them, demanding to be let alone to do as they please (Isa. 53:6). These illustrations suffice.

About five hundred years before Jesus, a spirit being withheld an angel God had sent to Daniel for three weeks. Later, Satan, Judas, the Pharisees, Herod, Pilate, and Rome allied to kill Jesus (1 Cor. 2:8, compare Deut. 4:19, Ps. 2:1–3, Luke 22:1–6, John 18–19, Acts 4:25–28, 17:30, Rom. 1).

In the present, God-defiant earthly and heavenly forces, visible and invisible forces, work around the clock, trying to separate believers from the love of Jesus. Typically, the forces chant, "Look for down moments in the lives of believers in our enemy. Stir and keep stirring memories of shattered dreams, rejections, hurts, and wounds; memories of traumas, abuses, and pain and the like, as proof that God is a killjoy, not a joy giver, and you'd sidetrack many of them."

They get busy accordingly (Rom. 8:35–39, compare Eph. 6:12).

In the future, there will be a repeat of the spirit-human alliance that killed Jesus. Only this time, it'll be led visibly by Satan. The satanic alliance will fight the fulfillment of redemption in Jesus (Rev. 20:7–10). But like the one before it, this alliance too will fight self-defending and lose self-defeated (Rev. 20–22).

Childlike trust and dependence on God equal freedom from God-defiance, the satanic principles of defiance, force, greed, selfishness, and evil ambition. While God-defiance holds on to self-in-control, childlike trust and dependence on God surrender control without regrets, worries, or despair.

That's foolish trust in God. It's spiritual, moral, mental, and emotional alignment with God and God's purpose. The alignment makes us channels of what God is doing, making the miraculous works we do, the ones God is doing.

That was how Jackie, a twenty-two-year-old British woman, whom we shall meet later, left home without support from a mission or church organization or financial resources. She went to the Walled City in Hong Kong, convinced that God would provide for her and protect her while she sought to bring wholeness to drug addicts. And she saw many addicts saved, healed from addiction, and restored to wholeness through prayer alone.

Carol experienced similar wholeness in Pasadena, California. But in her case it was after twenty years of fruitless medical and clinical treatment. I knew the facts after I'd prayed for her for two years.

Two years earlier, Carol and I exchanged "Hi" on a flight of steps leading from outside the building to the students' center on Fuller campus. She was coming down the stairs. I was going up. As we passed each other, I felt nudged to pray for her. I didn't know what about, why, and how, or for how long.

I picked up her name the next day through eavesdropping. A month later, I overheard Carol tell a friend in the mail room she was dealing with a rape aftermath. That piece focused my prayer for Carol.

Another time, at the students' center, I again overheard Carol tell some friends that her rape was incest.

That broke my heart and intensified my prayer for her. On and off, I fasted and prayed for Carol, foolishly trusting God to come through for her in a way only he could.

Two years later, I heard hurrying footsteps behind me in an empty hallway. "Excuse me," a voice said beside me. It was Carol.

"Hi," she said.

We kept walking.

"Hi," I said.

"My name is Carol."

"I'm Wilson."

"I'd like to talk to you some time. When can I see you?" Carol said.

We scheduled to meet in a week at a nearby park.

"The grapevine led me to you—" Carol said when we met.

"Huh?" I said.

"I have a rape problem that's killing me. For twenty years I've seen doctors, counselors, and therapists. I've also been to support groups and faith healing places. But I still have it. I don't know what else to do. Can you help me?"

As she talked, I prayed silently, asking God if I should tell her I've been praying for her for the past two years. I had clearance in my spirit. So I told her. At that, Carol broke down and cried like a baby. Then she said, "You didn't know me. Yet you loved me enough to pray for me for two years, amazing."

Carol started weeping again. And she wept for a rather long time. When she stopped she said, "You're the first person who ever loved me."

"I don't know about that," I said. "Your mom and dad must have loved you more than that."

"My mom might. But she's an alcoholic. My dad . . ." Carol stopped and sobbed. "If he loved me, why did he rape me, he and my brother, two weeks apart?"

"I'm sorry. How old were you?"

"Ten."

Silence engulfed us for fifteen minutes. Then Carol spoke up, smiling. Her light blue eyes sparkled.

"Do you know something? I'm feeling better already."

"You are?" I said.

"I'm not the lie I've believed for these many years."

"What lie?"

"All my life I thought I was worthless, convinced that no worthwhile person would be raped by her dad and brother. What a wicked lie. I don't believe that anymore. I'm free, ha."

Carol jumped up and stood. She walked three times around the bench on which we sat, humming a tune. She sat back down, beaming joy and peace. Then she said, "Listen. If I were worthless, God wouldn't ask a total stranger to pray for me." She stared at me and continued. "You've prayed for me for two years without knowing me. God is awesome."

She stopped and closed her eyes, her back flat against the backrest of the bench.

Five, ten, twenty, minutes later she opened her eyes, looked at me and said, "Let's pray. I want to thank God."

First, she thanked God for making her unique and precious and for saving her. Then she thanked God for caring so much for her that he'd led a total stranger to pray for her for two years. And he'd led her to meet the total stranger face-to-face.

When she stopped, I prayed, thanking God for the privilege to be involved in what he was doing in Carol's life. And we packed up.

In three weeks, Carol had changed from a shy-looking, fragile person to a brazen, bubbly person. Her doctors and counselors confirmed her total recovery but remained clueless about how. What a story.

But the story behind the story was this. I recklessly loved Carol, a total stranger, and foolishly trusted God to come through for her, while praying dumb prayers about that.

The simplicity removes this whole thing out of the realm of spiritual gifts. Instead, it places foolish trust in God, reckless love for people, and dumb prayers in the domain of family likeness. We do what our Father does since we are his children.

According to Peter (2 Pet. 1:3–11), these pieces came with everything that's ours in our birth into the kingdom of God. Receiving them obligates us to guard, feed, and exercise them. Their balanced development grows us in Jesus-likeness. Jesus modeled how from the cradle.

SECTION FOUR: HAPPY BIRTHDAY

CHAPTER 7

When Angels Celebrated Birthday on Earth

A vast crowd of angels praised God, saying, "Glory to God in the highest, and on earth peace among men with whom he is pleased!" (Luke 2:13–14). The crowds of angels praised God to celebrate the birth of Jesus on earth. An angel had just announced his birth to shepherds watching their flocks at night nearby.

To them he'd said,

> I bring you good news of a great joy which will come to all the people; for to you is born this day in the city of David [Bethlehem] a Savior who is Christ the Lord. And this will

> be a sign to you: you will find a babe wrapped in swaddling
> cloths and lying in a manger.
>
> (Luke 2:10–12)

The shepherds went to check it out. They returned "glorifying and praising God for all they had heard and seen, as it had been told them" (Luke 2:20).

About two years later, magi arrived in Jerusalem, looking for the newborn king. They went to King Herod to find out about him. Herod himself wasn't helpful, but a court priest disclosed that prophecy had predicted Bethlehem as the birthplace (Matt. 2:1–6, compare Mic. 5:2). The magi located the baby Jesus and worshiped him, giving him gifts of gold, frankincense, and myrrh (Matt. 2:9–11).

Unlike the magi, King Herod was outraged. He sent soldiers to kill every male child two years and under in and around Bethlehem, and it was done (Matt. 2:16–17). But Jesus was not one of them. God had forewarned Joseph to escape to Egypt with him and Mary moments earlier (Matt. 2:13–15).

Why would the birth of Jesus celebrated by angels, shepherds, and magi outrage a Judean king? To the extent he killed many infants believed to have included Jesus?

John, and Isaiah before him (Isa. 7:14, 9:6–7), had said that the birth of Jesus was a cosmic event. In it, the invisible Word of God, which God used in creating the created order, became human (John 1:1–1–5, 14–18, compare Col. 1:15–20). The angel Gabriel had said to Mary,

> The Holy Spirit will come upon you, and the power of the Most High will overshadow you; therefore the child to be born will be holy, the Son of God (Luke 1:35). Then Mary said, paraphrased, "The Spirit is doing it, you say? That settles it. I'm ready."
>
> (Luke 1:38)

The role of the Holy Spirit continued to unfold. Mary went to visit her cousin Elizabeth, who was then six months pregnant with John the Baptizer. At Mary's greetings, the baby John turned in Elizabeth's womb. At once, Elizabeth was filled with the Holy Spirit. And she exclaimed, addressing Mary,

> Blessed are you among women, and blessed is the fruit of your womb! And why is this granted me, that the mother of my Lord should come to me? For behold, when the voice of your greeting came to my ears, the babe in my womb leaped for joy. And blessed is she who believed that there would be fulfillment of what was spoken to her from the Lord.
>
> (Luke 1:39–45)

What a baby shower! Elizabeth and Mary were actors and spectators at the same time. As actors, six months' pregnant Elizabeth opened the door to welcome her cousin Mary who'd dropped in for a visit. But suddenly, Mary's greeting changed the women from actors to spectators, as they watched God's plan unfold.

Mary's greeting caused Elizabeth's baby to turn in her womb, filling Elizabeth with the Holy Spirit. And Spirit-filled, Elizabeth acknowledged Mary's baby as Lord. She commended Mary for believing angel Gabriel, who had announced to her the mysterious conception of Jesus.

Mary replied with a song of praise she sang as she composed it. She praised God for making her the mother of Messiah. For the moment, both ladies basked in the awe of the power and presence of the Holy Spirit.

Thirty years later, the Holy Spirit descended on Jesus. And God the Father audibly said, "You are my beloved Son; with you I am well pleased" (Luke 3:21–22, compare Mark 1:9–11). Later, Jesus publicly announced his job description in terms of the Holy Spirit,

"The Spirit of the Lord is upon me, because he has anointed me to give life to the spiritually bankrupt; to free those ravaged by sin, God-defiance, (i.e. defiance, force, greed, selfishness, and evil ambition); to give sight to the spiritually blind; and to inaugurate entrance into the kingdom of God."

> (Luke 4:18–19 paraphrased,
> compare Isa. 61:1–2).

Jesus would die, resurrect, ascend to heaven, and be enthroned, in the Spirit (Rom. 1:4, compare Luke 22:29, Eph. 1:19–23).

What for? The one by whom, through whom, and for whom all things were made (Col. 1:15–20) became human that repentant sinners can know God. Once born physically like us, he grew up like us. And once born spiritually like him, we too grow up like him. Angels celebrated his birth on earth. Do angels celebrate our spiritual births also? If so, where and why?

CHAPTER 8

When Angels Celebrate Birthdays in Heaven

Angels celebrated on earth the birth of Jesus on earth (Luke 2:10–14). But they celebrate our birth into the kingdom of God in heaven. "I tell you," Jesus said "there is joy before the angels of God over one sinner who repents" (Luke 15:10, compare verse 7).

And like Jesus' birth, our birth into the kingdom of God is totally the work of the Holy Spirit. To Nicodemus, a Pharisee, Jesus said,

> Truly, truly, I say to you, unless one is born anew, he cannot see the kingdom of God . . . unless one is born of water and the Spirit, he cannot enter the kingdom of God. That which

is born of the flesh is flesh, and that which is born of the Spirit is spirit.

(John 3:5–6)

How thrilling—my spiritual birth occurred here in the physical world, in Ghana, in fact. But it rippled to the spiritual world. Angels celebrated it. And while God gained a child, Satan lost a victim. "He [God] has delivered us from the dominion of darkness and transferred us to the kingdom of his beloved Son, in whom we have redemption, the forgiveness of sins" (Col. 1:13–14, compare John 1:12).

Yet the day it happened was as ordinary as any other. Late afternoon, the second Thursday in March, Mom took me for a walk in a coconut grove at the east end of town. I had just turned ten. Mom stared at me as we walked along and said, "Son, do you know God in a personal way?"

Anyone but Mom could ask me that question because Mom, more than anyone else, knew that Sunday was the high point in my childhood week. I was in church before the third and last church bell tolled at 9:30 A.M. When it stopped, it said the pastor and choir were at the door to the sanctuary. The congregation stood to receive them.

The choir, robed in black gowns with white collars for ladies and hip-length white surplices for men, proceeded into the sanctuary. They walked down the center aisle in two lines, singing, "Jesus shall reign where'er the sun . . ." The pastor followed three paces behind them, robed in clericals.

Five paces before the altar, one line veered left, circling the altar clockwise, and the other turned right, circling the altar counterclockwise. The lines merged into the first six pews in front to the right near the organ, standing.

The pastor stood in front of the altar, facing the congregation. Hush. Then he trumpeted a psalm. The choir responded with a doxology and sat down. The congregation followed. Usual rituals took their toll and the choir and pastor recessed, singing heavenward again. The worship service ended. I ached for next time.

Did Mom, in a keen mother fashion, catch the ache and its meaning and effects on a religious son? Was that why she asked, "Do you know God in a personal way?"

She must have. Unsatisfied with my answer, she went ahead and told me how, using Nicodemus (John 3).

"Nicodemus was a ruler of the Jews, a teacher of the scriptures and a good man," Mom began. "But Jesus told him, 'You must be born spiritually to live spiritually.'"

I thought, *That means, aside from my ten-year Christian upbringing, I too need to be born spiritually to live spiritually.*

"How?" I asked.

"As human beings," Mom said, "we're all prone to want to be let alone to do as we please. That's what it means to be human. And that's what makes us all sinners, because all our acts of sin come from that. Do you understand?"

"Yes, no, eh, no. Tell me, Mom."

"Wanting to be let alone affronts God, our Maker," Mom said. "It's telling God we own our lives. We know what life is all about. We know better. We don't need God."

I thought. *How can anyone not need God? What can we do right without him? We all need God, all the time.*

"Mom," I said, "that's bad, very bad indeed. What can we do about that?"

"Repent for being like that," she said. "And believe that Jesus died so that you won't die, that is, live eternally without God, for being a sinner."

"I do with all my heart," I said.

"Good. Now, ask God to forgive you and free you from the hold and dirt of sin."

I pictured the "hold" and "dirt" of sin as being trapped, helpless and hopeless. It's nice to know that God wants to do something about it. But I wasn't sure he would.

"Mom," I asked, "are you sure he will?"

"Certainly," she said. "God did not only promise he would. Right now, he's waiting to forgive you, free you and, enter your life. Accept his forgiveness and welcome him into your life. Trust him. He means business. And he enters your life the moment you ask him."

Just like that, huh? There was no lightning or thunder when I did. But instantly I knew a peace and freedom I'd never known. The next few days I devoured Mark, Luke, Matthew, and John, with new meaning and delight. Seven months later, I shared the experience with my dad. He experienced God the way I did right then. Three days later he died.

Initially, his sudden death shocked and saddened me, and maybe made me angry with God. But right then, a passion to nudge church people (Dad was) to be sure they know God in a personal way seized me. I climbed trees and rooftops at dawn, sang, and preached two-minute sermons.

Sometimes when I climbed down, I met people gathered to check out if I were an angel. Sharing the joy, peace, freedom, and power found in a personal relationship with God became a lifestyle for me ever since.

My study of the Bible later showed me that I had been expressing the life, freedom, and power that people receive when they enter a personal relationship with God. Biblical examples are numerous.

Filled with life, freedom, and power, the woman Jesus met at Jacob's well in Sychar, Samaria (John 4:1–42), went and brought her townspeople to Jesus. The exorcised legion demoniac went to ten towns and told how Jesus had freed him and given him life and power (Mark 5:1–20).

Similarly, Zacchaeus (Luke 19:1–10) instantly decided to give back money he'd stolen from people through inflated taxation. And Mary Magdalene supported Jesus financially from the time he exorcised her of seven demons and saved her (Luke 8:1–3, John 20:1–18). This endless list shouts a resounding message.

God's life in people is like a house on a hilltop. It can't hide. Neither can it drown or fizzle out in people who truly receive it. But for recipients to remain Jesus-like in foolish trust (Luke 18:17, compare Heb. 5:7–10), reckless love (Matt. 5:43–48, compare John 15:13), and dumb prayers (Heb. 5:7–10 and Matt. 9:37–38), they have to mature the Jesus-likeness in them. Only then can they reflect Jesus better and work Jesus' works after him, as he promised.

In this also Jesus set them an example in crawling unembarrassed.

Section Five:
Ridiculous Crawling

CHAPTER 9

When God Crawled
Unembarrassed

Born as an ordinary human baby, Jesus grew up like one. He sat on Mary's lap. Joseph held him in his arms. He played with neighborhood kids. Luke said he "grew and became strong, filled with wisdom; and the favor of God was upon him" (Luke 2:40).

At twelve, he went to the yearly feast of the Passover in Jerusalem with Mary and Joseph. But he disappeared when the feast ended. Mary and Joseph concluded he might have gone back to Nazareth with his peers, not a strange assumption for a twelve-year-old. But they were mistaken. He wasn't home when they got there, so they returned to Jerusalem.

After three days' search, they found him in the temple. He sat with the sages, listening to them and asking them questions. They were amazed at his understanding and his answers (Luke 2:41–47). Mary and Joseph didn't know what to think.

"Son," Mary said. "Why have you done this to us? Your father [meaning Joseph] and I have searched for you everywhere."

"Sorry about that," Jesus said. "I thought you would know that I would be in my Father's house" (Luke 2:48–49).

Mary and Joseph didn't understand that either.

However, Jesus returned to Nazareth with them and was obedient to them. He grew up to be a fine young man, full of wisdom. God loved him. And so did all who knew him (Luke 2:51–52). When he turned thirty, he joined the crowds John the Baptizer was baptizing in the Jordan. And he was baptized as well.

But something happened to him that didn't happen to the others. After his baptism, as Jesus came up out of the water, the heavens opened and he saw the Spirit of God descending like a dove and settling on him. And a voice from heaven said, "This is my beloved Son with him I am fully pleased" (Matt. 3:16–17).

That put Jesus at the spot where Adam and Eve stood in the Garden of Eden (Gen. 1:26–31). As with Jesus, God was pleased he'd appointed Adam and Eve as rulers of all the created order (verse 31). But Genesis 3 says Eve and Adam wrecked it shortly afterward. They chose to rule unaccountable to God instead of ruling under God. What would Jesus do, standing at the exact spot?

The Spirit drove him to the desert to decide. Then Satan came along. He enticed Jesus to defect from God, just as he'd done with Eve and Adam (Luke 4:1–13, compare Gen. 3). He enticed Jesus to choose to use his power to self-serve.

If Jesus did, he would be formed in God-defiance just like Eve and Adam. At once, he would lose the chance to expose Eve and

Adam's God-defiance, namely, defiance, force, greed, selfishness, and evil ambition. And he would also lose the chance to defeat it. Then he forfeits the opportunity to launch God-dependence which is self-imposed weakness, childlike trust and dependence on God, love, prayer and being Spirit-led.

Jesus rejected Satan's offer. He chose to stick to the original intent, to be God-dependent, though he was the Word of God by whom, through whom, and for whom all the created order, both heavenly and earthly, human and spiritual, was created (John 1:1–5, Col. 1:15–20, compare Heb. 5:7–10).

The Hebrews passage says,

> In the days of his flesh, Jesus offered up prayers and supplications, with loud cries and tears, to him who was able to save him from death, and he was heard for his godly fear. Although he was a Son, he learned obedience through what he suffered; and being made perfect he became the source of eternal salvation to all who obey him.
>
> (verses 7–9)

Jesus faced premature death attacks not less than five times (see Matt. 21:23–46, Matt. 22:15–46, Luke 4:16–30, John 7:53–8:59, and John 10:31–39). He could have used his power to defend himself, but he didn't. Instead, he prayed, depending on the Father to rescue him when and how he saw fit (see chapter 1).

And the Father rescued him on that basis, godly fear. And like ordinary people, he was exhausted and hungry (Matt. 21:18, John 4:6, Mark 4:36–38). He wept (John 11:35), and he felt crushed with grief (Matt. 26:38). He even asked for prayer (Matt. 26:38).

Jesus learned to trust and depend on the Father through suffering (Heb. 5:8). And perfected, he became the source of salvation to all who obey him (Heb. 5:9).

But why did Jesus have to be born a baby and grow up like one? Hebrews 2:14–18 answers:

> Because God's children are human beings—made of flesh and blood—Jesus also became flesh and blood by being born in human form. For only as a human being could he die, and only by dying could he break the power of the Devil, who had the power of death. Only in this way could he deliver those who have lived all their lives as slaves of the fear of dying . . . .

That means, identification with us aside, Jesus had another agenda when he was born and grew up human. Only in human form could he, his eternal nature notwithstanding, die. And only in dying to resurrect could he defeat Satan, sin and death, and their controlling power on people, and free the repentant from their enslavement to that power (Heb. 2:14–15, compare 1 John 3:8).

In Jesus' own words, "No one can enter a strong man's house and plunder his goods, unless he first binds the strong man; then indeed he may plunder his house" (Mark 3:27). The "strong man" is Satan, the ruler of this world (2 Cor. 4:4, compare 1 John 5:19). And Jesus is the "stronger-man," who had indeed defeated Satan to free us from our lifelong bondage to the fear of dying.

That's why Jesus is our sole freedom from the power of Satan and the power of the fear of dying (Heb. 2:14–15).

Emphasizing these truths, Revelation 12:11 says we overcome Satan through our redemption in Jesus and our bold witness to Jesus, on pain of death if need be.

So in his birth and growth process, Jesus identified with us to defeat Satan and deliver us. In our spiritual birth and growth process, we identify with Jesus to experience him and his victory. Our experience of both aligns us to God and his purpose.

When he tugs or nudges us, we respond as ready vessels of and for his life, joy, peace, freedom, and empowerment to people who belong to him and to those who don't.

Jesus insists that believers in him need a growth process for that to happen. "If you continue in my word, you are truly my disciples, and you will know the truth, and the truth will make you free" (John 8:31–32).

What does that mean, really?

CHAPTER 10

When Adults Crawl Delightfully

There's that moment when God suddenly breaks in to repentant people. In a split second he recreates them from the heart. He imparts his life to them. And in that instant they're born spiritually (2 Cor. 4:5–6). They begin a spiritual existence alongside the physical. Because it's genuine, it has four witnesses.

First, God orders a baby shower in heaven. Second, the converted knows he or she has entered a personal relationship with God. Third, Satan knows he's lost another victim to Jesus, not that he knows the exact victim he's lost. And fourth, with time, people around the recreated one would see a life of beauty that could only be explained in terms of God.

That glorious beginning of a personal relationship with God changes our lives from the inside out, conforming us to the likeness of Jesus, but only when we let it transform our thought and behavioral patterns (2 Cor. 5:15, Titus 2:11–14). The transformation is our growth process. As Jesus took human baby steps, then we too take spiritual baby steps. With delight?

In an earlier quote, Jesus told Jews who'd believed in him, "If you continue in my word, you are truly my disciples, and you will know the truth, and the truth will make you free" (John 8:31–32, compare 1 Pet. 2:1–3, 2 Pet. 1:3–11). That's Jesus' invitation to the believer's growth process, taking spiritual baby steps.

The dialog and climactic act that immediately followed that invitation focused on the need for the growth process.

"I tell you the truth," Jesus said, "all people need to be freed from the power of sin. And only the Son of God gives that freedom" (John 8:34–36).

"We don't," the Jews said. "As Abraham's descendants we're already free" (John 8:41, compare verse 33).

"Ah, you're missing the essential thing," Jesus said. "To be children of God, all people, including Abraham's descendants, need to exercise childlike trust in God. Abraham himself did. And God counted it as righteousness to him" (John 8:37–40, compare Gen. 15:6).

"You are missing something," they said. "We, Isaac's descendants, unlike Ishmael's, are the true children of Abraham. That makes us children of God. Get that?" (John 8:41).

"If you were children of God," Jesus started, "you wouldn't be seeking to kill me. That isn't like Abraham. It's like Satan. He, in fact, is your father" (John 8:42–47).

"Witch hunting, Jesus, witch hunting," they said. "You're demonized, that's why" (John 8:48).

"I'm not demonized," Jesus said. "I speak on God's behalf. Do what I say and you'll live" (John 8:49–51).

"Imposter," they said. "You're out of your mind claiming to be bigger than Abraham and the prophets" (John 8:52–53).

"The prophets talked about the Son of God. That's me. Abraham knew that. And he was glad he did" (John 8:54–56).

"Liar," they said. "You're not yet fifty years old, and you have seen Abraham?" (John 8:57).

"I tell you the truth," Jesus said. "Before Abraham was, I am" (John 8:58).

"Blasphemy, blasphemy, stone him," they said and rushed on him to lynch him (John 8:59).

How could they? A moment ago they believed in Jesus. A moment later, they're ready to kill him. All that blindness, deception, and hostility would have remained concealed if Jesus hadn't pushed for commitment to a growth process as proof of belief.

That is precisely what makes the believer's growth process critical. It consists of belief, discipleship, the truth, and freedom (see passage above, John 8:31–32). The hub is "belief." And "discipleship," "the truth," and "freedom," layer on, onion-fashion. It's the only way believers become Jesus-like.

Belief (verse 31a)

Belief is faith that saves. Faith saves only when it's trust and dependence on God alone to save, forgive, reconcile, and give eternal life and the Holy Spirit. Only through faith does God establish a personal relationship between himself and the repentant, forgiven, and reconciled person.

When faith doesn't translate into childlike trust and dependence on God, watch out. It becomes childlike trust and dependence on human reason, expressing itself in faithlessness, unbelief, disbelief, and skepticism toward God, God's Word and God's Spirit (see chapter 6).

Like those Jews, we might believe "right things." But we'd be blind and deceived about their limitations, flaws, and biases. We don't see it or admit it when those biases, flaws, and limitations eclipse God, God's Word, and God's Spirit, stunting our faith and growth. That's tragic. But discipleship prevents the tragedies through exposing and eliminating them at the roots.

Discipleship (verse 31b)

Discipleship, at least informal discipleship, isn't new to us. We habitually apprentice our parents and peers, teachers and pastors, and heroes and community. All those apprenticeships give us certain identities with their respective sets of values, motivations, aspirations, and behaviors.

Our spiritual birth gives us a new identity, an in-Christ identity. It too has its own set of values, motivations, aspirations, and behaviors. It's only fair that we apprentice the giver of our new identity as we do the givers of our other identities.

Our prior identities derive from defiance, force, greed, selfishness, and evil ambition, Eve and Adam's legacy to the human race. They focus on self-dependent, or independent behavior. Not so our in-Christ identity. It focuses instead on God-dependent behavior. Precisely, it comes from Jesus.

Jesus modeled God-dependence through giving up his right to be equal with God (see chapter 9). He learned to trust and depend on God as a servant without rights, doing and saying only those things the Father did and said. Finally, he died like a criminal to save lost humanity. But he resurrected as God, now enthroned over all rule and authority and all power and dominion (Phil. 2:5–11, compare Eph. 1:19–23).

In discipleship, Jesus' followers learn to be deliberate about self-imposed weakness (Phil. 2:5–8), childlike trust, and dependence on God and prayer (Heb. 5:7–10). It would follow that they learn to give up comfort and pride in social, racial, ethnic, professional rights, privileges, and advantages that hinder them from worshipping God single-mindedly and serving people lacking those rights without intimidating them.

Like Jesus, they learn to hold power and position lightly. They learn how not to self-seek or self-serve.

From Jesus they learn to deepen their love for God until it's deeper and stronger than their love for self and family, acceptance, recognition, and possessions. Only from Jesus can they learn to accept and care for all believers, irrespective of their backgrounds, and to love and pray for people who treat them like dirt (compare Matt. 5:43–48, Mark 12:29–31, Luke 14:25–35, John 5:19, 30).

And only from Jesus can his apprentices learn to pray, surrendering self-will and personal agendas, and committing to the will of God and his agenda. Even so, prayer becomes a lifestyle only when his apprentices learn to submit to the leadership of the Spirit, as Jesus did. Then the Spirit motivates, sustains, and directs praying (John 4:23–24, Eph. 6:18). That positions Jesus' disciples to experience the truth—Jesus himself—better and deeper.

The truth (verse 32a)

In getting to know the truth, we get to know Jesus himself. Jesus is the way, the truth, and the life (John 14:6). Why? Our claim to have eternal life is measured in terms of our knowledge of Jesus and the Father. "Eternal life," Jesus said, "is to know the only true God, and Jesus Christ whom you have sent" (John 17:3).

But "No one," Jesus said, "knows who the Son is except the Father, or who the Father is except the Son and anyone to whom the Son chooses to reveal him" (Luke 8:22). If Jesus had left this matter here, he's to blame for our lack of intimate knowledge of himself and the Father. But he didn't. He told us the basis on which he does the choosing.

"Whoever has my commands and obeys them, he is the one who loves me," Jesus said. "And he who loves me will be loved by my Father. I too will love him and, manifest myself to him" (John 14:21). Jesus reduced "my commands" to "a new commandment."

> A new commandment I give to you, that you love one another; even as I have loved you, that you love one another. By this all men [people] will know that you are my disciples, if you have love for one another.
>
> (John 13:34–35)

Put together, we love (accept and care for) one another as proof of our love for, and obedience to, Jesus. Loving one another shows the world that we belong to Jesus. Delighted, Jesus reveals more of himself and of the Father to us, in us, and through us. Why?

For one thing only Jesus unconditionally loves good and bad people, both elite and outcasts. Therefore, unconditional acceptance and care for others in spite of their backgrounds stands as the loudest and clearest evidence that Jesus makes a difference. He indeed frees people from bondage to divisions, hate, and violence that derive from satanic principles of defiance, force, greed, selfishness, and evil ambition.

The freed do become Jesus-like.

Freedom (verse 32b)

Freedom in Jesus divides into two. First, it frees us from the pull of rights, privileges, and advantages that societal satanic principles of defiance, force, greed, selfishness, and evil ambition lavish on people who say "yes" to them.

Second, freedom in Jesus helps us to give our "yes" to God, God's Word, and God's Spirit instead. Freed, we live joyful, peaceful, and zestful in spite of any consequences of that yes (compare Luke 11:23, 14:25–35 and 2 Pet. 1:1–11).

Like Jesus, Paul, and Peter, to name but these, experience would teach us we're blessed indeed when freedom in Jesus brings us in conflict with the way things have been, when, like everyone else, we too said yes to the rule of satanic principles, and no to God, God's Word, and God's Spirit.

> Blessed are you when people insult you, persecute you, and falsely say all kinds of evil against you because of me. Rejoice and be glad, because great is your reward in heaven, for in the same way they persecuted the prophets who were before you
>
> (Matt. 5:11–12)

> Indeed all who desire to live a godly life in Christ Jesus will be persecuted.
>
> (2 Tim. 3:12)

> If you are insulted because of the name of Christ, you are blessed, for the Spirit of glory and of God rests on you.
>
> (1 Pet. 4:14)

And why not? Balanced growth in belief, discipleship, "the" truth and freedom makes us Jesus-like. Therefore, everything that hates him would hate us. And all that love him would love us (John 3:19–21, compare John 1:5, 1 John 1:5).

Then in us, as in Jesus, the Spirit has freedom to blend his fruit of love and gifts of supernatural abilities for victorious living and effective witness (1 Cor. 13:1–13). We become sensitive to the Spirit's tugs and nudges, to serve as vehicles of God's goodwill, wholeness, fullness of life, joy, and peace to people and situations just like Jesus served.

SECTION SIX:
TUGS AND NUDGES

CHAPTER 11

When God Tugs and Nudges People

God calls some to be prophets and apostles, priests and pastors, evangelists and missionaries. But he tugs and nudges all his children. The tugging or nudging is always outside their gifting, expertise, and experience. Why?

The tugs or nudges don't invite the tugged or nudged to do the mundane that flows out of their comfort zones. No. Rather, they invite people to do the extraordinary. Those tugged or nudged have to trust God foolishly or it won't work. They'd have to extend themselves to the limit, to recklessly love someone or a situation, or it wouldn't happen.

Often, there are obstacles and hindrances to overcome. Hundreds of "what ifs" buzz all around. Self-doubt erupts like a volcano. It spills lava, screaming, "This is insane, impossible, unprecedented, unconventional, or presumptuous." The heat scorches attempts to pray while mocking efforts to trust and depend on God.

A Jewish slave girl faced the heat in Syria. She was a house servant to General Naaman, commander of the army of the king of Syria, the world power of the day. Crossing the master-slave chasm to obey God's tugging on her heart looked ridiculous, impossible.

But when she did, she connected her master to the prophet Elisha, who healed him of his leprosy. Through the healing, the Syrian commander became a worshiper of God (2 Kings 5:1–19).

Hannah's obstacles were equally daunting. They were:

- her society's stigma, labeling barrenness a punishment from God himself
- her rival's ridicule
- her husband's inability to either enter her pain and shame, or hush her rival
- high priest Eli's poor judgment and mockery

How dumb to pray in a context like that. But when Hannah fasted and prayed, hoping against hope, she became the mother of Samuel, a non-Levite, who replaced Eli and his sons as priest and judge (1 Sam. 1–3).

Then there was Mordecai. He felt tugged to motivate Queen Esther to speak out for the Jews. But he also knew that the imperial decree to annihilate all Jews was irrepealable. Esther's fear for her life was also legitimate. She could die for appearing before King Ahasuerus uninvited.

But Mordecai went ahead, nonetheless. And when he called for fasting and prayer as Esther requested, the impossible happened.

Haman, the mastermind behind the decree, died on the gallows he'd built for Mordecai. King Ahasuerus empowered Mordecai and Esther to issue another imperial decree that authorized Jews to defend themselves. And unknown to King Ahasuerus and even Mordecai and Esther, they rescued not only the Jews. They also preserved the promises and hope of the coming of Jesus (see the book of Esther).

Similarly, Philip faced Jewish condemnation for stopping in Samaria. Jews hated Samaritans. On the other hand, Samaritans might reject him for the same reason. Therefore, convincing Samaritans that, though a Jew, he loved them was but the beginning. They had to feel loved. Then they would open up to him and what he had to say. He couldn't make them. Everything shouted, "madness."

Yet when Philip talked to them about the outrageous love of Jesus and worked Jesus-like miracles as well, the results were phenomenal. The legendary occultist Simon and his towns-people converted to faith in Jesus (Acts 8:1–13, compare John 4:1–42).

Then there were Priscilla and Aquila, wife and husband. They felt nudged by God to help Apollos fill in the gaps in his theology. But an intellectual and social chasm stood between them and Apollos. Apollos was a learned man and an eloquent speaker. They were tanners.

But when they crossed the chasm, the results were again phenomenal. The church in Ephesus adopted Apollos as its missionary to Achaia.

> [The church in Ephesus] wrote to the believers in Achaia, asking them to welcome him [Apollos]. When he arrived there, he proved to be of great benefit to those who, by God's grace, had believed. He refuted all the Jews with powerful arguments in public debate. Using the Scriptures,

he explained to them, "The Messiah you are looking for is Jesus."

(Acts 18:27–28, compare verses 24–26,
Rom. 16:3–4, 1 Cor. 16:19)

What does that say? Whenever the tugged or nudged obey, they act contrary to reason. But the results always exceed anything they could imagine, meaning that acting non-reasoning isn't acting without sense.

The sense that guides the tugged and nudged is wisdom in childlike trust and dependence on the "tugger" and "nudger," who is God, and in intimacy with God. After all, tugs and nudges are body language between loved ones, not strangers or enemies. Enemies pull and push instead.

Therefore, it's intimacy with God, not gifting, that helps the ordinary person discern his tugging and nudging. Sometimes tugs and nudges come through something we hear or read, notice, or feel.

We're certain it's God drawing our attention when the effects invoked, as said earlier, are jolts of compassion, not pity; righteous outrage, not condemnation; or an impossible personal need, not a want.

The tugging or nudging needn't be dramatic, but it's strong enough to invite prayer. While praying, we might bump into someone or something that adds a piece here, a piece there to the puzzle. Other times, scriptural texts that scream, "Let God be God," like the following, come to mind. They demand foolish trust in God:

> Go and announce to them that the kingdom of Heaven is here. Heal the sick, raise the dead, cure those with leprosy, and cast out demons. Give as freely as you have received.

(Matt. 10:7–8)

You are witnesses of these things. And behold, I send the promise of my Father upon you; but stay in the city, until you are clothed with power from on high.

(Luke 24:48–49)

All authority in heaven and on earth has been given to me. Go therefore and make disciples of all nations, baptizing them in the name of the Father and of the Son and of the Holy Spirit, teaching them to observe all that I have commanded you; and lo, I am with you always, to the close of the age.

(Matt. 28:18–20, compare Rev. 1–3)

You [plural] did not choose me, but I chose you and appointed you that you should go and bear fruit and that your fruit should abide; so that whatever you ask the Father in my name, he may give it to you.

(John 15:16)

Truly, truly, I say to you, he who believes in me will also do the works that I do; and greater works than these will he do, because I go to the Father. Whatever you ask in my name, I will do it, that the Father may be glorified in the Son; if you ask anything in my name, I will do it.

(John 14:12–14)

Or God may give us an impression on the mind, a hunch, a thought, or an insight about the particular problem or situation. "What you are to say will be given you in that hour," Jesus promised when persecution prompts an explanation for loyalty to Jesus. "For it is not you who speak, but the Spirit of your Father speaking through you" (Matt. 10:19–20). How much more would the Spirit act through us when God cues, tugs, or nudges us?

Therefore when added insight or information intensifies the
nudging or tugging—the burden—it's a signal to stay tuned.
It's also a signal to fast and pray like crazy because God wouldn't
burden us that much for fun (see Carol's case in chapter 6).
When the burden lifts, we know another miracle is here or it'll
soon be (see Harry's story in the Introduction).

God tugs and nudges ordinary people. But when they obey,
the results are always extraordinary. Why? God is at work,
working through everyday, ordinary people. Commander
Naaman's slave girl, Hannah, Mordecai, Philip, and Pricilla
and Aquila were typical. We'll soon see that Jackie Pullinger
and Heidi Baker are, too.

CHAPTER 12

When the Tugged and Nudged Move

By 1972, what later became known as St. Stephen's Society in the Walled City in Hong Kong had hundreds of rehabilitated drug addicts befriending the homeless and leading them to Jesus. But when the society, then a youth club, had barely started, gangsters vandalized and overran it.

A sixteen-year-old gangster told Jackie Pullinger, who was running the place, "We're poor. And here you come supported by a rich church in England."

Jackie told him she was there on her own without organizational support or a financial base. Did she convince him? Maybe not. However, Jackie restarted the youth club, attracting addicts from fourteen to forty. A gang leader volunteered to guard her and the place.

"Thanks," Jackie said. "But try Jesus. He's the only one who can free you from drug addiction."

"I'd like to," the gang leader said, "but I'm no good."

"You don't have to be. Come to him as you are."

One night, the gang leader slipped into the meeting. He stood in a corner all by himself and started to pray, his first prayer ever. All of a sudden, he started speaking in tongues. The addiction left him just like that. In a short time, he became a leader in the youth club.

Another gang leader came to Jackie and said, "We've watched you for four years and we realize that you genuinely love people."

"Thanks," Jackie said.

Then the gang leader said he'd become a believer in Jesus if Jesus would heal the most rotten addicts he had on hand.

"Bring them," Jackie said.

By that time, healed and rehabilitated drug addicts, prostitutes, and gamblers had learned instinctively to pray for one another. A group of them surrounded the new arrivals and prayed for them. One by one they were freed. And they received Jesus as their Savior and Lord afterward. The gang leader kept his word. He too received Jesus and was freed from drug addiction.

Sanga, one of the rehabilitated, said, "Change comes through being touched by the love of God. And once touched, you can't help but turn around and share it with someone else."

That was what sent the rehabilitated after the homeless. But it all began with Jackie, a twenty-two-year-old oboe graduate from the Royal College of Music in England. She went to Hong Kong with the conviction that "the same Jesus who helped the hurting and helpless would do the same today."

Today, St. Stephen's Society continues to cure drug addicts through prayer alone without the use of conventional methods.

Jackie's "patients" withdraw from drugs, totally free from the usual agony associated with abrupt quitting of the habit.

Like Jackie, Heidi Baker was a PhD, Systematic Theology, from King's College London. In 1995 she and her husband, Rolland, went to Mozambique to demonstrate Jesus' love to the worst of the worst delinquents and dropouts who lived off public dumps. They started with giving free meals and clothes, sharing their showers with the homeless.

At the time, Mozambique was in political turmoil. Government officials told Heidi and Rolland they were wasting time. Thugs broke into their home, stole and vandalized property. Heidi recalled being shot at five times.

Once, two pickup trucks full of gangsters, one in front of her and one behind, trapped her with a gun to her temple. All she remembered doing was to cry out "Jesus." And suddenly, she and her van-load of kids got out of the place. They made it home safe, but not for long. Gangsters put a twenty dollar contract on Heidi's life.

It seemed Heidi and Rolland weren't getting anywhere. They felt like quitting. Heidi said she was willing to go back home and work for Wal-Mart. Then she caught pneumonia. She returned home to treat it. She checked out of three hospitals, still dealing with a stubborn case of pneumonia.

She went to Toronto praying, "Lord, let me do some less stressful work for you."

She got healed of pneumonia while praying. In a vision she saw thousands of rejected and famished kids calling her "Mama, Mama." She protested that taking care of 380 of them had worn her out. How could she take care of thousands?

Then, according to Heidi, she saw Jesus, his eyes dripping liquid love.

He told her, "I died so that there will always be enough."

"Since that day," Heidi said, "I've never said no to any child."

She returned to Mozambique not only healed of pneumonia—she was also spiritually renewed with a deeper commitment to love the unlovely.

Heidi and Rolland bought Shahango, a slum that churches, governments and humanitarian organizations had ruled out as unredeemable. Through networking, North American volunteer medical teams came to help. So did builders. School buildings and dormitories shot up.

Little by little, education for those who couldn't afford it, healing for the sick, human dignity for the dehumanized, and hope for the hopeless grew and flourished and started transforming Shahango.

Since then, Heidi and Rolland have seen amazing miracles of healing for the blind, crippled, and those afflicted with AIDS.

Dr. Artah Singh was a medical doctor who once helped out at Shahango. Citing himself, he said that transformation at Shahango worked both ways. As a North American surrounded with abundance, he didn't know he was isolated from the needy. But seeing the grace of God touch and transform people has given him a deeper appreciation of the power of God.

"My prayer is," Dr. Singh said, teary, "God, break my heart with things that break your heart. Help me to feel the pain and hurt in the hurting."

Heidi and Rolland's Shahango became people-loving-people. "It's thousands loving thousands. That is the joy of rehabilitated Shahango," Rolland said.

Similarly, thousands and thousands experienced transformation when witch doctors in Kedame, Ghana, failed to kill me, and they ran to Jesus instead. I had challenged them to kill me to prove their claim to be more powerful than God. This happened at a campaign I'd organized in Kedame, the hometown of witch doctors Kyifie, Kpo, and Kamla, aged 105, 95 and 75, respectively. I was sixteen.

They had often bragged about their ancestors, who killed the first missionaries to their town with a spell. From time to time, they claimed responsibility for church feuds, plague-like sicknesses among church members, sudden deaths of church leaders, and high turnover of pastors in local churches. In that way they held the churches in town and other towns around hostage for over a hundred years.

Their power source was an aquarium in a basket. Rain and hurricane-resistant, it hung about a hundred feet in space above their courtyard at the west end of town.

Christians and non-Christians feared them, but they were popular for their ability to peek fifteen to twenty-five years into the future for seekers regarding family and finances, longevity, and security.

I fasted for ten days, right up to the beginning of the campaign. I had laryngitis and lost my voice. Therefore, I couldn't preach the first two nights. Just before I mounted the open-air pulpit the third night, one of the hosting pastors told me that those witch doctors were present. "Leave them alone," he said. "We want you alive."

I prayed silently and sensed that God wanted me to preempt them. So I especially welcomed them to the meeting from the pulpit. "Today is your day," I said. "Kill me in ten minutes just like your ancestors did those missionaries. Do it to prove that you're indeed more powerful than God."

After fifteen minutes I said, "Perhaps you need more time. Take the rest of the night." I closed the meeting.

At four o'clock the next morning, I was summoned to the shrine of Kyifie, Kpo, and Kamla. They showed me their aquarium in the basket. It had dropped, squashed, to the ground. The water had splashed, leaving the fish wriggling in the mud.

"It dropped last night," Kyifie said, "while we tried to kill you."

"Really," I said, amazed.

"Not only that," Kpo said, "we saw a wall of fire around you. It crashed every spiritual dart, hex, curse, and spirit we shot at you."

"A wall of fire, really?" I echoed to myself.

"Son," Kyifie said, "we want to worship your God."

Kamla and Kpo nodded in agreement.

"Burn down our shrine and everything in it, now," Kyifie ordered and led the way to it.

The flames attracted the townspeople. Those who had relied on these men for protection switched to Jesus. So did thousands within a twenty-mile radius.

Overwhelmed with awe, I wrote a song,

> I planned a campaign for ten days; it was too long for the Spirit. He cut it to three days. I planned it for a town; that was too small for the Spirit. He extended it to a twenty-mile radius.

The conversion of Kyifie, Kpo, and Kamla, their towns-people, and the thousands of people within a twenty-mile radius paralleled the conversion of Simon the occultist and his townspeople in Samaria two thousand years ago (Acts 8:4–13). The Holy Spirit used Philip, a deacon, then. This time around, he used a kid. Amazing.

Family likeness is life, God's life in ordinary people like Heidi, Jackie and me, and Philip, Hannah and Naaman's Jewish slave girl (see above). Because it's God's life, albeit in ordinary people, it's invincible. It can't be foolhardy or timid or complacent.

Rather, it's wise, bold, and sensitive to the tugs and nudges of God. It sees obstacles in the way, not as roadblocks, but as inevitable and motivational to trust God foolishly, love people recklessly, and pray crazy, doing dumb fasting if need be. Life begets life; it connects people and situations to the life source, God.

God's purpose is to make the family likeness—our lifestyle—a preview of things to come. What role do we play in making it our lifestyle for the long haul?

Conclusion:
When Family
Likeness Gushes Life

What would it look like, feel like, smell like, sound like, and taste like when good is severed from evil, joy from sorrow, comfort from pain, peace from struggle and war? Revelation 21:4, 21:9–22:21 say that's no fantasy. It's part of the distant future hope of believers in Jesus. That's why God went all out to be born in human form and grow up just like an ordinary person (chapters 7 and 9 above).

Does God have a preview of the future reality in the present? Yes, he does. There is indeed a peek of the future in the present. God wants the now church, groups of believers in Jesus, to make it so real that God-hostile human and spirit beings, Satan, and demons, can't miss it. (Eph. 3:10). God's showpiece in the present is his life, eternal life, gushing God-likeness in ordinary people.

Whenever God's life is imparted and received, angels celebrate it in heaven just as they did on earth at the birth of Jesus. It delights the Spirit, who oversees the new birth (chapters 8 and 10 above) when the family likeness gushes life in ordinary people.

They unnaturally naturally, trust God foolishly as God trusts, even when those he trusts betray trust (chapters 5 and 6 above); love recklessly as God loves outrageously (chapters 3 and 4 above); and discern God's tugging and nudging and pray when it makes no sense to, just as it makes no sense that Jesus and the Spirit should pray (chapters 1, 2, 11, and 12 above).

Jesus used several imageries to describe the family likeness. One of them is abundant life. "I came that they may have life, and have it abundantly," Jesus said (John 10:10).

The abundant life is the "thirty, sixty and hundred times what had been planted" in the fertile soil in the parable of the sower (Mark 4:8). It's the "army of people" that evolved from scattered bones, to skeletons, to lifeless bodies, to living persons in Ezekiel's vision (Ezek. 37:1–14, compare Ezek. 36:25–27).

Jesus also calls abundant life gushing rivers.

> On the last day of the feast, the great day, Jesus stood up and proclaimed, "If any one thirst, let him come to me and drink. He who believes in me, as the scripture has said, 'Out of his heart shall flow rivers of living water.'" Now this he said about the Spirit, which those who believed in him were to receive; for as yet the Spirit had not been given because Jesus was not yet glorified.
>
> (John 7:37–39)

The Holy Spirit produces abundant life in repentant people. Everyone who comes to Jesus, repenting of having lived independent of God, receives forgiveness and new life as a free gift (Rom. 6:23, 2 Cor. 5:17). And he or she is reconciled to God. God's Spirit, who oversees the spiritual birth, also oversees the spiritual growth into Jesus-likeness (Eph. 4:1–32).

Freedom and joy, peace and contentment now dance where bondage and anxiety, fear and greed have been. God knows it when it happens. He orders a celebration in heaven (Luke 15:7, 10, 22–24). Satan also knows he's lost another victim to Jesus (Col. 1:13).

And of course, the converted know it in terms of an inexplicable aliveness (John 9:25, 2 Cor. 5:17). So do close associates. They see it and are curious about it, but they can't deny it (Mark 5:1–20, John 4:1–42).

Gushing life turned the woman Jesus met at Jacob's well at Sychar in Samaria into an instant evangelist. She went and brought her townspeople to Jesus (John 4:1–42). The former legion demoniac went to ten towns and told how Jesus had exorcised him and transformed him (Mark 5:1–20).

Zacchaeus decided to give half his income to the poor and to return four times over what he'd stolen from people through inflated taxation (Luke 19:1–10), all showing that abundant life under the leadership of the Holy Spirit is robust, zestful, winsome, and contagious.

John 7:37–39, cited above, describes abundant life as a surging river. It

- pushes debris off the shore
- keeps its waters fresh and clean
- sustains life within it, and
- waters vegetation along its entire course (compare Mark 5:1–20 and John 4:1–42).

Kaye, a banker in Ghana, told me her experience of that reality. We sat in a corner of the sanctuary after I'd given a talk at a

Sunday afternoon Bible study in her church. She said she read the Scriptures with new meaning. She couldn't stop singing in her heart and out loud sometimes. She exuded contagious joy, her colleagues said. Then tragedy occurred. She said, "I married a man I shouldn't have. I thought I could lead him to Jesus."

"Hmm," I said.

"I couldn't. He rather converted me to his ways," Kaye said. "I gave up daily devotion, prayer, church attendance, and personal evangelism and discipleship. Wild parties and heavy drinking ran our lives. Then I had our first child. The second came a year later. Two years after that, the third arrived. Ten months later, my husband took off and left us. He went somewhere in the USA."

Kaye gasped and continued.

"That was when the worst happened. I blamed God for letting this happen to me. I plunged into heavier drinking to drown all memory of God."

"Did it work?"

"Six years I've tried without success."

Kaye stopped and wept for a while.

"I need out," she said. "Please help me."

We scheduled to meet at her house in two weeks. But a week before our meeting, Kaye's last born and middle children died six days apart.

When we finally met, we studied John 7:37–39 (see passage above).

"Kaye," I said, "since you know the surging river imagery of abundant life, let me paint three perversions of it for you. And please tell me which one describes your present condition."

"Okay," she said.

The first is a suffocating river. It's choked, stagnant with garbage and undeposited silt in most parts. The fouled, muddy, smelly waters, infested with parasites, drip through rotten debris at the bends. The river strangles fish and frogs and spits them out on the surface and riverbanks as meals for vultures, crows, flies, and maggots.

The second is a struggling river. It's dried up in parts and pooled muddy and stinking in other parts, the hangout of foul water-loving pests like moss, mosquitoes, and dragonflies.

The third is a sandy riverbed. Smooth stones, pebbles, and sand over which waters glided in the past are now stripped. The entire riverbed is dry, strewn with dead and dried-up fish, and withered scrubs, ferns, or reeds. Here's the has-been river.

"How pathetic," Kaye said, sighing.

"Pathetic?"

"I've been there, done that with all of them."

"Tell me about it."

Kaye pulled a couple of Kleenex from a box on the end table. Then she said, "This is all hindsight. Thanks for your descriptive sketches of the perverted imageries of the flooding river. When I abandoned the surging river, I became a suffocating river. I cursed often and ridiculed church attendance, Bible reading, and prayer. I slid into a struggling river state without seeing it." Kaye blotted tears from her eyes.

Then she continued. "I had frequent nightmares fighting dragons, crocodiles, and snakes in muddy waters. I woke up panting, drenched with sweat. Now I think I'm a sandy riverbed. I've tried suicide, counseling, and therapy. Nothing worked. I've returned to church, cynical, stark, and with insomnia and emptiness. I tell you, it hurts." Kaye wiped tears from her eyes again.

"Ah," I said. "I have good news for you."

Her light brown eyes widened. I read surprise mixed with delight in them.

"Yes," I said. "It's the identity recovery message Jesus sent the churches in Ephesus, Pergamum, Sardis, and Laodicea. He asked them to 'remember,' 'repent,' and 'return'" (Rev. 2:5, 2:16, 3:3, 3:19). We turned to the passages and read them.

"Kaye," I said, "since you've remembered abandoning the surging river, repent for abandoning it and return to it with all your heart. Your river of life will flood again."

Kaye did. She radiated joy and peace that weren't there a moment ago. To answer her question, "How do you keep your river of life flowing?" we studied Ephesians 6:10–20 for the next six weeks, referring to 2 Corinthians 10:3–5 and Colossians 3:12–14.

> Stand therefore having girded your loins with truth, and having put on the breastplate of righteousness, and having shod your feet with the equipment of the gospel of peace; besides all these, taking the shield of faith, with which you can quench all the flaming darts of the evil one. And take the helmet of salvation, and the sword of the Spirit, which is the word of God. Pray at all times in the Spirit, with all prayer and supplication. To that end keep alert with all perseverance, making supplications for all the saints.
>
> (Eph. 6:14–18)

At the end of the study, Kaye said, "I now see the spiritual armor as a lifestyle. It characterizes people who stay alive in Jesus."

"Right," I said.

We boiled the characteristics of that lifestyle down to:

- truth: sincerity, genuineness, and transparency
- righteousness: clean conscience and pure motives
- peace: joyful contentment in Jesus
- faith: childlike trust and dependence on God
- salvation: assurance, comfort, and confidence of being saved by grace and kept by grace
- word: fed and trained by God's Word

- prayer: constant communion with God, surrendering control and personal agendas to God, and committing to his (compare 2 Pet 1:3–11)

Ten years later, Kaye became a pastor of the Nazarene Church of Ghana. Her son became an evangelist about the same time.

An abandoned wife and mom, bereaved of two kids less than ten six days apart, making an evangelist of the surviving kid while becoming a pastor is commendable. But that's a by-product of Kaye's recovery of her God-given identity in Jesus as a believer with family likeness.

When it's vital, it makes us:

- genuine and authentic representations of Jesus
- credible and Spirit-led witnesses for Jesus
- useful and usable to the Spirit
- sensitive and responsive to the tugs and nudges of the Spirit

Then, indeed, God's life in us aligns us with God, making us channels of his love, forgiveness, peace, joy, life, freedom, and wholeness, to people and situations. We work Jesus' works after him as he did the Father's.

And like Jesus, we too know the abiding presence of the Father. "He who sent me is with me," Jesus said. "He [hangs out with me because] I always do what pleases him" (John 8:29).

Further Reading

I list the following resources for further reading for this reason. Like *Family Likeness*, they invite us to take our in-Christ identity as seriously as God does.

Fresh Wind, Fresh Fire, Jim Cymbala **www.zondervan.com**

Mama Heidi, Eric Velu Productions **www.visionvideo.com**

Not I but Christ, Stephen F. Olford **www.Olford@memphison-line.com**

Prayer Power Unlimited, J. Oswald Sanders **www.christianbooks.com**

Proclaiming the Good News, Stephen F. Olford **www.Olford@memphisonline.com**

Pursuit of God, A.W. Tozer **www.amazon.com**

Repenting of Religion, Gregory Boyd **www.bakerbooks.com**

Soul Survivor, Philip Yancey **www.zondervan.com**

The Conflict, Wilson Awasu **www.airleaf.com**

The Gospel Unplugged, Rich Wagner **www.gospelunplugged.com**

The Jesus I never Knew, Philip Yancey **www.zondervan.com**

The Law of Love, Contracts International **www.visionvideo.com**

The Myth of a Christian Nation, Greg Boyd **www.zondervan.com**

Tozer Devotionals, A.W. Tozer **www.cmalliance.org/res/tozer**

Transformational Conversion, Wilson Awasu **www.pleasant-word.com**

To order additional copies of this title call:
1-877-421-READ (7323)
or please visit our Web site at
www.winepressbooks.com

If you enjoyed this quality custom-published book,
drop by our Web site for more books and information.

www.winepressgroup.com
"Your partner in custom publishing."